Foreword

A few years ago, *Lectio Divina at the School of Mary* was published, a work originally written in 2001. The teaching of Lectio Divina began in 1995 and has continued to develop since then. Over time, a significant challenge emerged: many individuals noticed that the daily readings often conveyed the same message. The Lord was beginning to impart His supernatural light, with the Holy Spirit acting directly and personally.

However, the light people received seemed general rather than specific, practical, or precise. As a result, Jesus' will often appeared unclear, leaving people uncertain if they were truly listening to Him or practicing Lectio Divina correctly.

The key was to persist in prayer until the light became clear and Jesus' will certain. This crucial aspect, however, was not sufficiently emphasised or explained in the first book. Therefore, the purpose of this new book, *Finished and Unfinished Lectio Divina*, is to assist all who have begun practicing Lectio Divina, as outlined in the first book or in the Solid Foundations Course, and need clarity on this issue.
Additionally, articles published on the website have been included in this book.

One important caveat: while reading this book, you may find it challenging—and it is—but it's essential not to forget the fundamental role of the Holy Spirit in Lectio Divina. Yes, we must make a sincere effort to listen to Jesus, and yes, we must rely on the general help of God's grace to help us hear His voice. However, we should always remember that when we offer ourselves to the risen Lord, or when we renew this offering, He bestows upon us His Holy Spirit, enabling us to truly hear Him.

If this book encourages us not to underestimate our effort or the importance of expressing our will to listen to the Lord, it is equally important that we do not lose sight of the Holy Spirit's role as we read each page. The process of listening is a collaboration between our effort and the Holy Spirit's guidance. The purpose of this book is to help fine-tune this collaboration, with a particular focus on our part in it.

I- Finished and Unfinished *Lectio Divina*

A Bit of History

It is in 1999, at the request of Micheline, that I first wrote about *Lectio Divina*. In fact, after my lesson on *Lectio* she asked me if I had any written material on the topic. At that time, I did not have anything prepared. Also, I was aware that the form of *Lectio Divina* I was presenting -based on the two readings- was relatively unknown, and I had not found a book that explained it in the detailed manner in which I had understood it since early 1983. Before that, in 1986, while discussing *Lectio* with a fellow Canadian Carmelite novice at Montpellier, I noticed with dismay that he seemed lost during our daily hour of *Lectio* practice from 8 to 9 a.m. This led me to an intuitive realisation: one day, I would write about *Lectio Divina*. However, this insight was soon forgotten.

I first taught *Lectio Divina* in 1992 during a retreat I was giving to my friend Daria at the same convent in Montpellier, but still, nothing was written down. It was not until Micheline's request in 1999 that I felt a strong sense of obligation to put down something in writing. In a single night, I drafted twenty-one pages -though poorly written- that would eventually become Chapters 1 and 2 of the published book and also form the content of the CTS book.

I share this story because, at that time, my understanding of the steps of *Lectio Divina* was framed around two crucial moments represented by two key demands/prayers and Jesus' responses:
1) "What do you want from me, Lord?"
2) "Help me to achieve it."
Of course the Holy Spirit was invoked. These two demands/prayers were illustrated in a twofold diagram showing Jesus being assumed to

be above, illustrating our intellect, our will, the gap between them, the arrows of each prayer, and Jesus' responses.

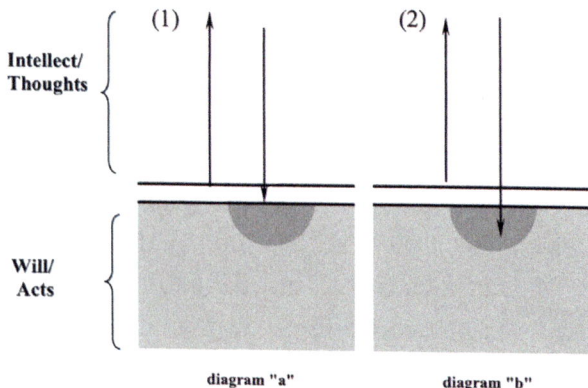

diagram "a"   diagram "b"

When the book was published, starting from 2003, I was discerning seven steps for the practice of *Lectio* (Not the actual three phases with fifteen steps that later evolved):

1. Sit down in a quiet and solitary place - in the morning if possible.
2. Ask the Holy Spirit for help in listening to the Lord.
3. Re-read the two texts until they reveal one single light for today.
4. Ask for the strength of the Holy Spirit in order to put the light received into practice.
5. Write down briefly the light received.
6. Put into practice the word received today.
7. Verify at the end of the day that we have incarnated the word, and give thanks to God for it.

In the seven steps of *Lectio Divina*, the core elements are steps (3), (4) and (6).

The first key moment (3) involves the initial demand (the first upward arrow), where I ask the Lord, "What do you want from me?" His response reveals what He desires for me to do or change in me today (the downward arrow, lightly touching the will).

The second crucial moment (4) is the subsequent demand (the second upward arrow) where I ask the Lord to give me his Holy Spirit to help me put His guidance into practice. Jesus' reply, is God's grace flowing downward and entering my will, helping me put into practice what He said (the second downward arrow, entering the will, touching a specific area, the act to perform).

It goes without saying that the goal of these two moments is to put into practice what Jesus has said (step 6).

For me, *Lectio* is what the Lord relentlessly says in the Gospel: listen to me and put what I say into practice. It is the core of the Gospel. This is how we build our house on the rock of Jesus' Word (see Mt. 7), this is how we make sure our prayer is sound ("why do you call me 'Lord Lord' and don't do what I say" (Lk. 6:46)).

Since 1995, I have continuously taught *Lectio Divina*. However, during my time teaching in Legnano, Italy, from 2004 onward, I was surprised to discover that many people struggled with implementing the practice. They often found themselves stuck at a specific stage in experiencing God's light.

I had always assumed that Jesus' first reply was clear and straightforward (represented by the first downward arrow), that when He answered our question "what do you want to me to do today" it was clear. However, through my experience in Italy, God revealed to me that the process of listening was more complex, that practising *Lectio* was not straightforward and "easy" for people. I learned that receiving Jesus' light involves more than one phase, each with its own intricacies. Many individuals seemed to be stuck in the process of discerning Jesus' message (see diagram below). The paradox is that they were making substantial progress: the two texts intersected at a certain point, they already had one light coming out of the two texts (see diagram below). This was really positive, it showed that the beginning of the supernatural action of the Holy Spirit had started. The light however was *general*, so they were unsure of what in practice Jesus was asking them to do and so lacked clarity and certainty. To find out that one can be blocked in the middle of the process, especially after having had the two texts saying the same thing (i.e. allowing the same Light to go through), was a significant realisation for me. I discovered that what I had previously viewed as a single, straightforward process was actually composed of differentiated steps. At least two. As one can see in the diagram below, the arrow is comes to a halt in the middle of its journey inside the mind.[1]

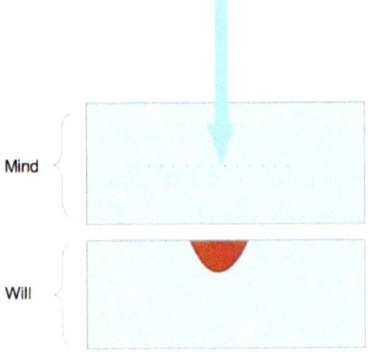

Witnessing that one can be stuck in the middle of the journey of descent of the light, witnessing that in fact this new step stage was emerging in front of my eyes meant that I had to do something. I was able to see that even if a light was received, it was still general, and Jesus' will was still unclear. It meant that the process of begging, asking, and insisting had to resume, until the light was clear, until Jesus' indication was clear, until His will was clearly expressed. This new stage had to be underlined in the teaching and consequently in a new Summary of the steps.

Today I may say that the first stage of the descent into the mind is the result of a first effort in our practice of *Lectio*, in the way we **offered** our ***mind*** to the Lord. Then the second stage where the light needs to reach the edge of the will, showing practically and clearly what was needed to be done, seemed to involve a more powerful and complete gift of ourselves to Jesus, where the ***will*** was clearly **given** to Him,

---

[1] Subsequently I realised that the majority of people have this experience. This is why my advice for each person wanting to implement *Lectio* is to check it, so they do not stay stuck. Often, but not always, I find that people are stopped by this difficulty, and they do not know what to do. Seeking help is needed.

freely, totally, unconditionally, with total trust and abandonment in His hands. We will see this illustrated below with Our Lady.

This insight led me to develop a more detailed framework, expanding from the original *seven* steps to *fifteen*. In this new approach, I differentiated between various types and depths of "reading" within the process of listening. One key point in these fifteen steps, is in the second part (Part II - Listening), in the distinction between the four forms of reading the sacred text: Read (1), Read (2), Read (3), and Read (4). Contrary to the over simplified and very widespread four-step model of *Lectio* of today: Read, Meditate, Pray, Contemplate, where "reading" might be seen as merely an initial phase, reading itself is an ongoing process, with ever deeper levels. In fact, we continually engage with the text, much like a person contemplating an icon stained glass, waiting for the divine light to reveal itself through them. We persistently read and re-read the texts until the Lord highlights in each text the passages He wishes to use to communicate his light to us. The supernatural light is given but it is *general*. Then, we keep reading, especially the highlighted passages in each text until the light becomes *clear*, *practical*, *certain*. The new insight I gained back then involves the distinction between steps 8 and 9 in this expanded framework (in the former one they comprised *one* step, now they were *two*):

I- Preparing

1- Sit in a quiet place
2- In the presence of Christ; entering into my conscience
3- Consider His desire to speak to me
4- I choose Him again as my First priority
5- I give myself to Him, unconditionally

II- Listening

Active phase: seeking understanding

6- Read (1) in order to understand the text

7- Read (2) in order to discover Christ's will

8- Read (3) until I see only one light

9- Read (4) until the light becomes clear

10- Write down the words or sentences from the readings that touched me as they become highlighted in the individual text.

III- Realisation

11- Asking the Holy Spirit's help in order to put the Word into practice

12- Giving thanks, being immersed in Him

13- Putting into practice the Word I have received

14- Echoes during the day

15- At the end of the day: giving thanks

The innovation in the fifteen steps lies in the distinction between step 8 "Read (3)" and step 9 "Read (4)". Step 8 marks the beginning of the supernatural phase in *Lectio Divina*, signified by one light given to us by Jesus. A general light, coming through the two texts, entering in our mind. It indicates that with the help of the Holy Spirit, Jesus is beginning to enter our mind, our conscious mind. This represents a radical shift from the general light of faith we have (meditating), (6) and (7), to a more specific, personal intervention of the Holy Spirit in our intellect (supernatural listening) (8).

Meditation

To meditate is traditionally understood in the Church as the reflection of the mind on a text, using the general light of faith we have in us from Baptism. In step (8) in *Lectio* we have the beginning of the supernatural process of listening. The difference between spiritual meditation (the general light of faith) and supernatural listening (the direct personal intervention of the Holy Spirit, i.e. the Particular Help of the Holy Spirit) is radical.[2]

One can easily notice that in *Lectio* we never use the verb "to meditate". The reason is that what we are seeking is *listening to Jesus* directly and personally, not reflecting with our mind on the text and extracting ideas, trying to find by ourselves an application in our daily life.

In her autobiography, St. Teresa of Avila places "meditation" as the first form of prayer, and she is very clear: this form is not supernatural, i.e. the direct and personal action of the Holy Spirit is not involved in it. Meditating for her is making an effort with the mind, with the general light of faith, reflecting on a given subject, extracting some light from God. Here it is a human effort of the mind to read and extract some "light" from the text.

There is nothing wrong in meditating on the sacred text. We can call it "spiritual meditation". In this case we go from a to b, b to c and c to d, with our mind, but this is not *Lectio*. If some insist on considering *Lectio* to be a *spiritual meditation* on the sacred text, one will have then to differentiate it from the real *Lectio*. One is with *the general help of the grace of God*, a form of meditation on the sacred text, and another one (the one we have at the School of Mary) which is supernatural involving the direct intervention of the Holy Spirit.

Personally, for many reasons, I do not think it is advisable to make a *spiritual meditation* on the text and call it *Lectio*. The main reason is that *Lectio* is practised by the faithful who have a living relationship with Jesus, or who are starting to have one. Also, traditionally *Lectio* was always understood as involving *Contemplation*. And *Contemplation* is by definition supernatural. One can see it in the

---

[2] For the direct and personal intervention of the Holy Spirit, the *Particular help of the Holy Spirit* see the following articles on the School of Mary's website: "The Particular Help of the Grace of God in St. Teresa of Avila" and "St. Thomas Aquinas' Explanation".

widespread form of *Lectio* inherited from the Middle Ages, the four steps to *Lectio* being: *Read, Meditate, Pray, Contemplate.* *Contemplation* is the goal of *Lectio*. This shows that the practice of *Lectio* was understood as involving the direct and personal intervention of the Holy Spirit, i.e. *contemplation.*

Lectio is first and foremost a liturgical experience where the Sunday Reading of the Old Testament is illumined by the Gospel's proclamation. In this sense there is a movement going from the first Reading to the Gospel and back again from the Gospel to the first Reading. This illumination of the Old Testament by the Gospel is the initial stage of *Lectio Divina*. This accounts for the mysterious reply of the father of all monks, St. Antony the Great, to the question: "how do you spend your day while working with your hands?", namely, "I go from the Old to the New and from the New to the Old [Testament]." St. Antony keeps doing this until the light becomes clear. This best illustrates the core occupation of the Monk: to "meditate day and night" on the Scriptures. *"Blessed is the man* [who's] *delight is in the Law of the LORD, and on His law he meditates day and night. He is like a tree planted by streams of water, yielding its fruit in season, whose leaf does not wither, and who prospers in all he does."* (Psalm 1:1-3) "Law" is understood as being the Sacred Text.

Meditation can be understood sometimes as a "ruminatio" (rumination), that is, a pondering and praying on the text until contemplation is given by God. It is more the work of the memory, where one repeatedly goes over the text or various texts in the mind. The process is akin to Mary's way according to St. Luke. *"But Mary treasured up all these things and pondered them in her heart."* (Luke 2:19 and 2:51) See for instance Fr. Matta El Meskeen (Fr. Matthew the Poor), "Orthodox Prayer Life", pp. 43s, 2003. See also Ghislaine Salvail, "At the Crossroads of Scriptures: An Introduction to *Lectio Divina*", 1996.

Going Deeper

Initially, the new light provided by the Holy Spirit to our intellect through the two texts is broad and general. For instance, the light can be on humility or mercy, or any other indication from the Lord. The initial light does not immediately clarify how to apply it in a practical way. The risk here is that we might take matters into our own hands, trying to implement these lights/virtues according to our own actual understanding.

It is crucial, however, to recognise that even when the Lord begins to speak to us, we must continue to ask and seek further clarity directly from Him. For instance, if it were "humility", we need to inquire: "Okay, humility—what does that mean in a concrete or visible way for me? How do you want me to apply it?" and all the while remaining open to the Lord's guidance. We should allow Him to reveal which specific area in us that day requires enlightenment, transformation, or purification. Which part of our will is ill and needs Jesus' power to be healed and made alive? The more we persist in our request and openness, the clearer the light becomes, eventually directing us toward a specific area wherein lies the action I will perform involving my will (Step 9). The light received is not general anymore, it is pointing clearly to some area in our will.

Note: When I check *Lectio* with people, I notice that often the temptation is that once the general light is given, i.e. once the two texts are saying the same, people take this general light and try to apply it by themselves in their own way. This deviation and human interference can be represented by the diagram below:

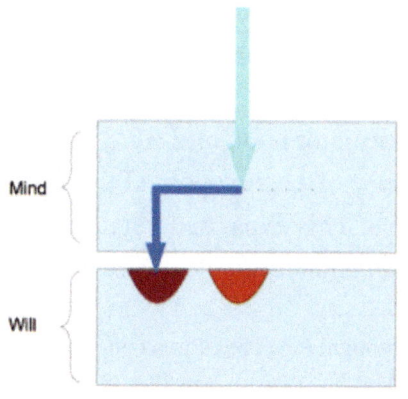

Note that this intervention stopped the descent of the initial light in the middle of its journey in our mind. Our interference is shown in darker blue, and the area we decide where to go with the general light and where to apply it, can be seen to be different (darker red). According to our experience and knowledge we are thereby taking the general light and conducting our own search as to where to apply it in our life. We are not following the precise indication of the Lord but are rather taking the light and trying to find an area, which ironically requires greater effort. This rushing into applying, rushing into forming conclusions is widespread and aborts *Lectio*.

Over the past twenty years, I have observed that transitioning from the general light to a more specific and clear light is a significant challenge for everyone, not just for my friends in Italy back in 2004. I have clearly seen that stopping the descent of the light in us right after receiving the general light prevents *Lectio Divina* from reaching its completion. When God begins to work in us and sheds His supernatural light upon our minds and when this process remains incomplete because of our intervention, I have referred to this as the "abortion" of *Lectio*. While the term is strong, it reflects the deep respect we owe to God and his action in us, not to mention the respect God has for our free will, and the necessity for our correct response and proper collaboration with the Lord's work: neither slower nor faster than Him. We need to be under his guidance.

As mentioned above, this insight into the step once we have God's response -and the continued effort required to allow the light to fully descend and touch our will- led to an additional teaching that is not fully developed in the earlier major book on *Lectio Divina*. Consequently, the *Vademecum* or *Summary* of *Lectio* evolved from having 7 to having 15 steps, as outlined above. This expanded version of the summary started to be included in the second edition of the book on *Lectio*.[3]

---

[3] The 15 steps are also thoroughly explained in a concise book I authored in 2012, in collaboration with Anna Maria Cattaneo, which is currently available in Italian and will soon be translated. In the meantime, English-speaking readers are able to find

Subsequently I have written an article entitled "Finished and Unfinished *Lectio Divina*" because I have frequently encountered this issue when people review their *Lectio Divina* with me. Reviewing or checking your *Lectio* with someone, then, is an important part of the process of learning *Lectio* (see the online article "Steps Toward Implementing *Lectio Divina*"). Since *Lectio Divina* is a practical exercise, checking its implementation often reveals significant insights about your own practice and helps ensure and discern when it works and what needs to be implemented. This is strongly recommended.

Many people -more than one can imagine- do experience the fact that the two (or three) texts of the Mass are saying the same thing to them, and this shows that the Holy Spirit has started to work within them and has started to introduce his light into their minds. However, the process of receiving this light is more complex and extended than one might expect, as the mind has various levels and functions. As a consequence, the descent of the light is a longer journey than people think.

As we have already said, often, the mind rushes into conclusions, interfering with and stopping God's work. This may happen out of ignorance of course. As a consequence, we get stuck at this first stage of the descend of the light of the Holy Spirit, not knowing what to do. The great number of cases having this difficulty shows that this issue has to be addressed extensively.

The following diagram shows the full journey of the descent of the light until it touches the edge of the will showing us, in the will, what "act" the Lord wants us to make. This is very different from stopping the light in the middle of its journey and trying by ourselves to apply it, our way. On the contrary if we continue to ask and beg, the light continues its descent according to Jesus' will, his way, and under his light. Nothing can equal direct and personalised guidance.

---

relevant insights in the online short article "Finished and Unfinished *Lectio*." This current article serves as a continuation of that discussion and of course goes further and deeper than the 2012 book.

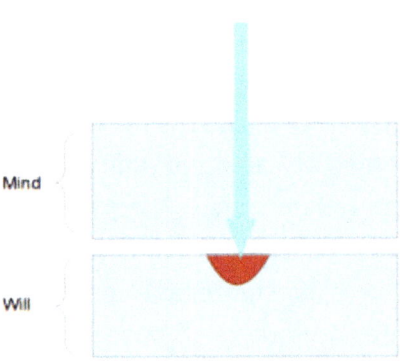

Mind

Will

The Act

First let us talk about what to expect, i.e. the *act* I am always mentioning. My approach to the "act" is probably unconsciously influenced by St. Thomas Aquinas' use of the word in the *Secunda Secundae* of his *Summa Theologica* (ST), when he studies human acts.

Far from desiring the reader to be inundated by St.Thomas' work or diverted from our subject, the chief concern of the latter remains the intervention of the Holy Spirit in us to reveal what act we should undertake. Briefly, then, the journey of the birth of a human *act* according to St. Thomas, from the mind to the will, is the following:

1- Intellectual Apprehension and Deliberation (ST. I-II, Q. 14, Art. 2),
2- Judgment (ST. I-II, Q. 15, Art. 1).
3- The Will's Choice (ST. I-II, Q. 8, Art. 1) "The will is a rational appetite, which chooses according to the intellect's judgment."
4- Execution (ST. I-II, Q. 1, Art. 1): Aquinas describes the execution of an *act* as the final stage where the choice of the will is translated into action: "The will moves the powers of the soul to the action which it has determined."

For me, when I use the word "act", as in an "act to make" in *Lectio*, I mean essentially: an inner transformative act made in collaboration with Jesus and his Spirit. He wants to change our will, because our will is ill, and He is the Doctor, the Divine Physician who knows us, knows what to heal, transform, purify in us. He knows how to transform the will in us that is ill, the will of the Old Man in us, of the Old Self, into his will, making/building the New Man in us, the new self, the new creature. It is an amazing work of collaboration where He is the one who knows best what to do and where to go. This is *Lectio Divina*: Jesus is building our new house (our soul) on the rock of his word (see Matthew 7:24-27). We are his dwelling place (John 15:4-6), we are immense. Our soul is immense. It shrinks of course because of sin, we lose some of his *likeness* and He has to enlarge us again at/to his infinite dimension.

Since our old self draws us to the outside world, we hear "act" as something to *go and get*, something in our external daily life *to do*. We look toward the outer world searching for something to do, but we are not aligned with his project, with his plan: He wants to transform us, and we think: *act* is something to do outside of ourselves. We diminish ourselves in fact to doers, to a robotic spiritual life where I receive an order and execute it. Easy. Maybe. But this is not God's way. Not God's plan. We are created in his image not in the image of another creature. We are created to enter into a personal, intimate relationship with Jesus, we are created to be his dwelling place, immense as He is! He is uncreated. So, who are we in his eyes? Expressed at its simplest, the aim of the Gospel is the evangelisation of *all* our being. This necessitates paying attention first to his work in our soul as if we were his garden. We are his garden. Consequently it would be illogical to expect Him in *Lectio* to ask us to do things exteriorly all the time. He wants to change us. Yes, it is true we live in this world and need to do things! But how do our acts begin? They always originate from within. This point is fundamental. The real change that will impact the world is the change within ourselves first. Jesus wants to make of us new creatures. This work takes time.

It is true that the first example I take of concretising the *act* are Jesus' words seems an external act: "go and reconcile with your brother" (Matthew 5:24). It is not. Yes, it is the most important, *the* universal example. It is at the heart of the Our Father: "[…as] we forgive" those who have offended us. But if we pay attention it will become clear that this act of forgiveness or act of mercy will have to originate in the soul, come from a change in the soul. The laboratory of Jesus is our soul. We need to look inwardly to find the *act*. For us to be able to forgive, we first need Jesus to heal our heart. To forgive, we need to receive from Him the Love He wants us to give to our brother. Note, all this is done while sitting and doing our *Lectio*. Did we move? No. Well this is an example of the *Act*! It is not an *act* like "go getters" will think it is. Of course, the exterior acts are never excluded from *Lectio*. I am just explaining exactly where the change occurs: it happens *in* the soul, in the conscious mind and in the conscious will. The *act* is *in* the will, *from* the will, *by* the will. But its starting point is given to the mind or intellect. With the help of the Holy Spirit, the will then executes what was shown to the mind, as will now be outlined in detail.

The Journey of Descent of the Light in Our Mind

Many people when they start to practise their *Lectio* based on the two (or three) Readings of the daily Mass, as I explain it, frequently find the common light, the common message. What is the real meaning of this? When the two sacred texts are miraculously used by the Lord to convey one thing to us this means that His Light, or if you prefer, the intervention of the Holy Spirit in the mind, has started. The Holy Spirit takes Jesus' Word for me today and introduces it into my mind.

But my mind is a big "factory", with four layers or ways of functioning at least. The descent of Jesus' message -Jesus' light- in us has to go through these four layers.

a) The first "layer" -the highest- in the functioning of our mind is the layer of *wisdom*: the mind is enabled by God's light to see everything, embrace everything with a general view, knowing how to order what we see, that is, seeing what should take precedence, what is more important than what. To reiterate, the light of the Holy Spirit here is perceived in its general capacity.

b) The following "layer" has more to do with the act itself of understanding: the intelligence of the thing itself. Intelligence comes from the Latin *intus – legere*, that is, to "read inside" of the thing, understanding it in itself. It seems abstract because we are studying the thing in itself: for example what is mercy? Here the mind sees its object (mercy for instance) in itself, penetrating it and seeing it from within itself.

c) The following "layer" is grounded more in reality, on the "scientific" level: we see how this can be applied in a practical way in real life practically in real life, how it would look, understanding how it could be applied. We are no longer in the theoretical contemplative level of what mercy is, we can already see examples of what mercy can be in daily life, in human life. It is more practical, but still general, i.e. not leading to something specific to do or change in us today.

We can represent the descent of the light so far as having reached the "middle" so to speak of the mind. See the diagram below.

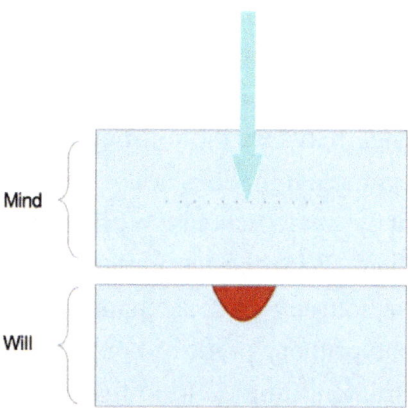

Mind

Will

d) Then comes the key level, the hinge between mind and will, the capacity of the mind to apply the light, to move toward the will, to look toward the will: this level of functioning of the mind **under the light of the Holy Spirit** shows how the mind can translate what it saw in the previous levels (that is, in general in wisdom, in intelligence in itself, and in applied cases), in a practical way in the will. This functioning of the mind helps us discover in the will what the Lord wants us to put into practice; it allows the light to descend into a specific, practical, here and now way, touching our will, not the will of others, touching what I can do, indicating it clearly (see diagram below). It is the Holy Spirit that makes the mind see under a clear light the particular act to perform. All our efforts should be concentrated on facilitating this descent of the light of the Holy Spirit until it becomes a clear act to perform.

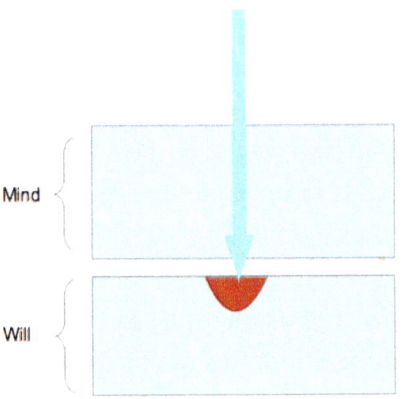

There is a huge difference between knowing in general what forgiveness is (it can be any other general light), and what it has to become for me today. It is the difference between the *general light* and the *particular light*, it is the difference between the journey through (a), (b), (c) put together and (d). The general light does not offer me a clear supernatural understanding of what the *act* to make is. While the particular light does. The difference is radical. With the particular light, we will be able to move forward, start a journey of real change, and start it in a very different way: from the primary point of contact, Jesus, and with clear guidance given by Him. Building a virtue first needs a new act, then it needs to be reinforced, by repetition. The first act is the most difficult one because it is the beginning and because it is totally new. It is only afterwards that repetition comes. First things first: the initial act. This is how the new self really starts to grow. Jesus knows us much better than any other guide, or self-help book. He knows our weaknesses. He knows from where we need to start, He sees things in us we fail to see, He knows the entire process because He *is* our way.

Spiritual life is a new life with Jesus. It exacts a deep change in us from the behaviour of the Old Man to that of the New Man. This is what is at stake. How can this change happen? If we look at who we are we find that the Old Man or old-self is taking up too much space in us. It has its own vision, means, goals, and ways.

This needs to change. Our will is ill, paralysed, needs healing. We need new acts, coming from Jesus. We need them to create a solid stable new way of behaving. Traditionally we call this a virtue. A virtue is the result of the repetition of a new act, this result being called a "new habit, a good habit". But how can we achieve this? The needed change seems insurmountable to us: we are weak, we have bad habits, but we are at a loss about where to begin. We do not know how to persevere. It is a real art, a divine art. Even if we have a book indicating to us all the new outlook we need to acquire (the new virtues), we do not know how to start, and how to persevere. We need Jesus' light, and Jesus' supernatural help: the direct and personal intervention of the Holy Spirit. This is where *Lectio* intervenes. *Lectio* here puts us in direct contact with our Guide, the Lord and his Holy Spirit. The uniqueness of what *Lectio* offers needs to be truly appreciated by each member of the faithful, and by each spiritual guide. We need to be very zealous about it, understanding its uniqueness and preserving it from any deviation. Let us go back to the radical difficulty we face with the necessity to change when we follow Jesus.

To illustrate what is at stake in this very important issue and how *Lectio* is the real powerful means at our disposal to employ for change, we can use a comparison: let us say that the needed change is about moving from an old place to a new place and that they are separated by a strong thick wall. It is imperative for us to move from the place where we are to a new place but how can we destroy this wall?! We then see ourselves as being in the place of illness and weakness, and that we need to move to the place of virtue, light, new life with Jesus. If we apply all our strength to destroy the strong wall, pushing with all our body, nothing will happen our strength being distributed over a big surface, for since the wall is very strong nothing will change. This effort is a *general* effort, and it is applied to the whole wall. It is like the resolution we take after confession, or after a retreat, or for the new year. A general resolution stays a general resolution. We are at loss, not knowing where to start and how to progress.

On the contrary, however, if we focus on one action only, and we put all our energy into it, if we drill a tiny hole in the wall, we will already be able to access the other side, we will be able to see the other side through this tiny hole. It seems *insignificant,* it is only one step, but it is a huge step, a necessary goal and newness will start to manifest itself. The light and vision from the other side of the wall become visible. Divine life is starting to be given to us and can start to flow. If this is achieved, we need to understand that from God's perspective we have really achieved something that day: we can "see" the other side through this tiny hole.

What the lowest level of the functioning of the mind (d) (see above) offers us is a unique practical understanding of God's light received in *Lectio*. The light and understanding of it are directed toward the will, toward crossing the abyss which separates the mind and the will. This last level (d) deals with the question: "Jesus, what am I supposed to do today?!" I am asking for the new act I never made before He needs to show me, the change He wants to realise in my soul. This is the level of "prudence" as understood by the ancients, or better said: the level of "discernment". As one can see, it aims toward one point! (the one point on the wall where we need to drill) Not two points! Not *our* opinion on how to apply the general light. Not a *general* effort, or a good general resolution like: "I will be merciful today". When we repeatedly beg and wait for Jesus' general light to reach the soil of our will ("on earth as it is in heaven") it becomes clear. The birth of the new act in the will, given and directed by Jesus as something we need to *see* in our mind, is daily work: give us "this day our daily bread" of your word is what we need to see in our mind. This way Jesus can hold us in his hands and transform us in his way.

Again, here the mind is looking toward the will, not *in general* but concentrating on letting the light move and become one act. The will is finally touched by Jesus' Word, and is transformed by his holy Spirit in/at one point only.

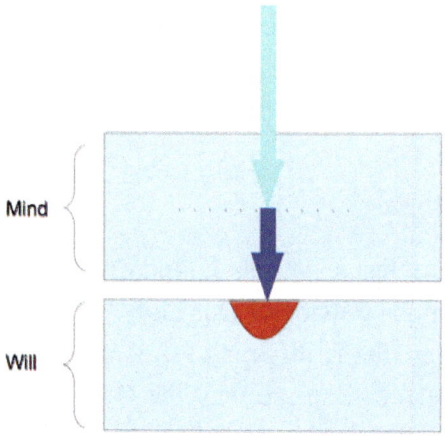

As we can see on the diagram above, the same light Jesus is giving to our mind, has a journey of descent: a, b, c, i.e. from clear blue (general light) to darker blue until it touches our will.

In spiritual life we need to use our mind. We need to put it in the hand of the Lord, we need to expose it to his Divine Light, to His Word. But we are not aware how rich our mind is, differentiated in its levels of activities, and we fail to realise that the descent of Jesus' light takes time from a very general view to a really practical implication for today. Taking time for the descent from Jesus' mind (heaven) to the concrete practical soil of our will is of the essence, which is the reason for *Lectio* taking at least one hour, and this descent needs our "facilitation", step by step: "Thy will be done on *earth* as it is in *heaven*". We contemplate your will O Lord, with our mind, and we let it descend into it until it becomes clear, and we can see how to apply it on the earth of our will. Again, to reiterate, it is imperative that we realise that our mind does not interfere in this descent. It facilitates. The difference is huge. We need to avoid intervening or interfering or deciding. This is very important. The Lord himself opens the way in our mind toward our will. He knows where He wants to go. All that we are required to do is to beg, to tell Him that we are open to his will; to put our will into his hands, again and again; to give Him full rein, allowing his light to descend, where He wishes it to, in the way He wishes; allowing his light to be shed on the area He desires and upon which he decides, and in the way He wishes it to be. This is why when He sheds his light on the will, one always has the impression of newness, the impression of: "oh, this, I would have never expected!" "Jesus surprised me, in the area I wasn't expecting". Or "Jesus showed me something I wasn't seeing", at least not this way.

Our Lady's Two Steps

Can the Incarnation of Jesus' Words happen without the Holy Spirit? Impossible. Can it happen outside of Our Lady? Impossible. Mary is our mould, the place[4] where the Holy Spirit forms us. But first, Our Lady is our role model. If we focus on the way the Word of God, the Second Person of the Trinity, became incarnate in Her womb, we find that there are two stages too in the Annunciation. When the Angel announces the Incarnation to Mary, that she will become the mother of the Messiah, even if the initial words of the Angel in the annunciation are true, they were not totally clear to her. As a consequence, she felt she needed to understand God's part and her part in the process more completely. She needed to know what she was supposed to do before saying "yes".

The Light is Initially General

"Do not be afraid, Mary, for you have found favour with God. Behold, you will conceive and give birth to a son, and you are to give Him the name Jesus. He will be great and will be called the Son of the Most High. The Lord God will give Him the throne of His father David, and

---

4 See this article : https://schoolofmary.org/our-place-in-god/ See also this article: https://schoolofmary.org/all-the-predestinate-are-hidden-in-marys-womb/ and this one: https://schoolofmary.org/our-place-is-in-marys-heart/

He will reign over the house of Jacob forever. His kingdom will never end!" (Luke 1:30-33)

Mary does not immediately say: *"May it happen to me according to your word"*. Why? As we have said, she lacked a clear understanding of it all. What the angel said was true, but Mary wanted more explanations in order to know what to do: *"How can this be,"* Mary *asked the angel, "since I am a virgin?"* (Luke 1:34)

God's Will Needs to be Clear

The same initial light we receive was first given to Mary and it will receive wider explanation and will be developed to include greater clarity, practical insight, something to do. Most important it will lead her to know what God wants to achieve in her and with her, and the part she has to play in it. The Angel's explanation will help Mary respond properly to God. Let us remember how God wants to treat us: *"I no longer call you* servants*, because a* servant *does not know his master's business. Instead, I have called you* friends*, for everything that I learned from my Father I have made known to you."* (John 15:15) Mary, indeed, is the first *friend* of God, the archetype of all Jesus' friends. God's desire is not for us to be passive recipients of his light, but would much rather we submit our minds to His Light in order to collaborate with Him, as his real sons, or brides. God could very well have given the entire light from the start, but it was not His choice to do so: Mary had to ask. Mary showed she understood what her dignity was in God's eyes, and wanted to understand and collaborate, as a real partner. Obeying God implies the fact that we first understand from within what He has in mind. The explanation the Angel gives to Mary is as follows:
"The angel replied, "The Holy Spirit will come upon you, and the power of the Most High will overshadow you. So the Holy One to be born will be called the Son of God. Look, even Elizabeth your relative has conceived a son in her old age, and she who was called barren is in her sixth month. For no word from God will ever fail.""

From these words we see that Mary understands her role of collaboration with the Holy Spirit. She just needs to offer herself to the action of the Holy Spirit for this very case. But she also learns from the Angel the impact of her act upon others who were unable to believe: Elizabeth and Zacharia (and all of us) who failed to believe, need Her to believe for them. So her yes" to the angel's words has a twofold consequence: a- the Incarnation of the Second Person of the Trinity and b- becoming the spiritual mother of all human beings, believing for them.

It is only then that she was able to make her act of loving faith and total surrender to God's project: giving Herself to God, to the Incarnate Word, to her mission at his side but also to her mission at our side. We are the mystical body of Jesus. So too Mary becomes the mother of not only the head but also of the body. *"I am the Lord's servant,"* Mary answered. *"May it happen to me according to your word."* (Luke 1:38) It is really admirable to see in Mary the archetype of the two steps of descent of God's light in us.

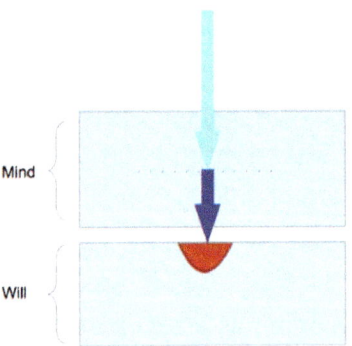

Mary shows us the way, and also teaches us how to listen to God in *Lectio*. She also helps us from within for God gives us her Heart, her mind, so we can really listen to Jesus her Son and do his will.
Luke shows us the workings of Mary's heart: *"But Mary treasured up all these things and pondered them in her heart."* (Luke 2:19 and 2:51) Pondering, reading, re-reading, pondering, understanding, praying, asking for clarity, until God gives us the clarity, is how we too must follow in Her footsteps.

Some people think that *Lectio* is a matter of intellect and that they are clever when they "get it" from the first light so that they do not need to spend that much time on *Lectio*. They rush into putting into practice the light without understanding it, without taking the right amount of time, without asking the right questions, needing more clarification. Here we have the Mother of God, with all her purity and holiness, who she still asks the right questions, seeking clarity to respond fully to God's will.

It behoves us then to learn from Mary, to ask Jesus to give us a heart like Mary's. Let us ask Mary to show us our dignity in God's eyes, and how the Lord wants to explain his will to us so that we can correspond better to it.

Two Things to Do

As we can see, the descent of Jesus' light has stages, and it can often stay general. We rejoice when the two texts are saying the same thing, we enjoy the "drunkenness" of seeing his intervention and realising his miracle of making the two texts say the same thing. Yet we tend to stop there trying to see by ourselves how to apply this light instead of continuing to allow the light to descend in us until it becomes clear. We might expect the light to be about some exterior work to do, while the Lord is aiming at healing our will. Far from our thinking is that the Lord will pinpoint something interior, something within us. We are not aware enough that the work He wants to realise is our inner transformation. This is the core of evangelisation. If the human being fails to change, if we ourselves fail to change, the Gospel itself fails in its very objective. We need to focus on ourselves, allowing His light to follow its path to our soul, to our will.

We need to continue to beg for further enlightenment by saying: "what does humility or mercy mean in practice for me? What do you want to change in me?" And very importantly, we must keep reading the highlighted areas of the text while we are seeking this clarity. We must never veer away from the texts. We must continue to go from one text to the other, focusing on the passages He highlighted, until He makes his will clear to us, until his light touches an/a specific area of our will.

So, two things at least are of paramount importance: begging and reading.

1- Offering our will anew to Him. It is as if at the first stage when we offered ourselves to him, to listen to Him, it was chiefly the mind which received the light. But now, we accept having a more in-depth relationship by renewing, we renew the gift of ourselves with a more complete act of love by offering our will, repeating to the Lord: "Here I am again, I don't mind what you do. Direct your light in me, to the area of your choice. I trust you, you never hurt, you come to heal me, you know me better than I know myself. I trust you Jesus totally; I trust you more than I trust my own judgement. You have free reign. Go ahead." This renewal of the gift of ourselves is a true act of love which allows the Lord to go deeper and touch our will. It is as if we offered Him our will. It is like the traditional movement of our hands when we pray the Our Father: we open them out, lift them to God, showing our total openness, our total surrender to Him. The hands often symbolise our will, so opening them out, raising them toward Him, expresses our renewed total surrender and entrustment. We open the deep door of our being to his action.

2- While doing this we keep reading. We never abandon the sacred text, because it is through the text that the Lord will talk to us, He will give the written words a new meaning, a power capable of penetrating our soul, capable of touching our will.

This is the phase of listening in *Lectio*. In a way it is the most difficult one, the most challenging one, because it is about allowing the Lord to enter freely within us. It is difficult because we need to enter into a real interaction with Him. Remember we are not servants or slaves; we are his friends. The difference is huge. The servant, the military obey orders. They do not interfere with the order it is in a purely robotic fashion. The individual's mind, his will, his life are not involved directly. While in the case of the friend confidence predominates for he listens to the deep thoughts of his fellow friend. He is invited into greater intimacy. This interaction involves the whole being and is infinitely much more demanding. Willing to engage fully with all our being with the Lord and renewing our commitment in the course of the process of listening, then opens the Door for the Lord to really enter: *"Here I am! I stand at the door and knock. If anyone hears my voice and opens the door, I will come in and eat with that person, and they with me."* (Revelation 3:20) Opening the door is the most challenging part! It depends on us, using the general help of the grace of God, and it is decisive because if we fail to do it, Jesus will not force the door! So, the bitter consequence that we often observe is that God seems to be silent in our life! Very committed Christians seem to deal with a silent God and the saddest aspect of this is that they do not know that the reason is that He is waiting, that His respect for our free will is that divine that nothing moves forward without our permission! It is the foremost responsibility of the Church to highlight this issue. It is the core part of its mission to explain to the faithful that God has no intention whatsoever of being silent. In fact, He gave us His Son, his Unique Son, proof of a divine infinite immense love for each one of us. His Son is His Word. God's Son teaches us to which extent He is yearning to talk to us in order to change us, purify us, transform us: thy will be done on earth as it is in heaven, therefore *"give us today our daily bread"* the bread of your word. He is clear on that: it is a real act of love to keep his commandments, to do what He tells us to do: *"whoever loves me keeps my commandments"* (John 14:21.23). He teaches us that it is not optional to love Him, but He cannot force us: *"you shall love God with all your strength, all your will, all your mind"*. And to love is to listen to Him and put what He says into practice, otherwise our acts do not originate in Him, He is not our real Guide and He will respond to these acts by saying: "Go away from me, I don't know you." But we will protest in reply: "I did miracles in your Name and prophesised in your Name, I did many things in your name," to be met by the stern rejoinder: "No, I don't know you, go away." (see Matthew 7:22)

31

It is by our not understanding the real practical insight of the Gospel that God remains silent, that our process of listening is uncertain. This is not God's will. Impossible. He did not give us his Son for the sake of uncertainty! This is a serious matter. He gave us his Son, his Word, His Words to change us. The process of the reception of these sacred redemptive Words cannot be undertaken randomly, with vagueness or with uncertainty. The process of our transformation is real, necessary and vital. The desire of God to talk to us, to heal us to transform us is immense. He really loves us therefore he is showing us, on a daily basis, what new inner act He wants us to perform. He gives us the capacity to do it, the Grace to do it. This is the essential function of the Holy Spirit: to make us hear Jesus' Word, to facilitate the incarnation of this Word, one Word at a time, one Word a day, for this Word to become alive in us. Otherwise, how can Jesus grow in us. This process requires interaction, time and space. It is a sacred process, not less sacred than the Incarnation or the Mass. In fact, it constitutes the first part of the Mass, the in-depth meaning of the Liturgy of the Word.

How can we live on earth with a silent God? With a silent or uncertain Jesus? Love on the Cross is not uncertain. He shed his blood. Nobody can doubt this. It is inconceivable that anyone can think that Jesus wants to be silent. It has the makings of a deep contradiction and a sin to think this. It is an immeasurable offence against the God who became incarnate and took thirty years to prepare (so to speak) and bake the bread of his Words that He then gave us during the three years of his public life. He came to give us his redemptive words, words that *are* Holy *Spirit* and Divine *Life*. He would be denying his very snature to deprive us of them! We cannot just fob it off lightly saying: "Oh lucky Apostles, they saw Him and heard Him speak." On the contrary, in the Mass the Priest and the Deacon (in the Eastern Rites) say the "Holy, Holy, Holy,.." before the Proclamation of the Word; they pray, invoke the Holy Spirit on the Assembly; they warn us and say: "silence, listen carefully and reverently." We have candles, incense, we take the Evangelarium (Book of the Gospels) in procession for what reason? Why all this? It is to show us that Jesus the Risen Lord is among us, and for three years (A, B and C, Sunday cycle), exactly as He did 2000 years ago, He will personally teach us. He is among us today, as He was 2000 years ago. Even better, because He is risen, and the Holy Spirit is given to us. God prophesied it in the Old Testament and said: "I myself will be their Shepherd" (see Ezekiel 34:15) and "I myself will guide them…" meaning that He would would feed them directly with His Words. Nobody can doubt the absolute/infinite desire of God to talk to us, to change us. This is why learning the process of listening and understanding the journey of Jesus' Word in us are crucial.

It helps immensely, after having understood clearly what He wants from us, to flesh it out, briefly, in our notebook with the date, and the feast if it applies, copying the sacred words which touched us, the ones He used to talk to us, and to write one or two sentences explaining to ourselves how we understood them. Seeing what the Lord has said to us in writing mirrors his Word to us and helps it enter our being more deeply and thereby encourages us to put it into practice.

Wrestling Like Jacob

Yes, *Lectio Divina* requires a total commitment to Jesus on our part. Yes, *Lectio Divina* requires a total involvement of our conscious faculties, at least the mind and the will.

In the second part of the 15 steps *Summary* of *Lectio Divina,* there are two phases: an initial phase described as the *Active Phase: seeking understanding*. In this phase we make an effort, with the general light of faith to understand the text. It can take some time and is normal and necessary. We are not used to the biblical world, culture, expressions, words, concepts. We can undertake some brief research, read footnotes, cross references, etc. Yes, this is an active phase, and it involves a certain amount of effort on our part.

The following phase is described as the *Receptive Phase*: the *listening phase: asking for the help of the Holy Spirit*. One might think that in this phase no effort is required of us, and that we just need to be receptive, and that it is preferable to simply wait for the Lord to intervene, whenever He wants and in the way He wants.

Yes, we pray, yes, we ask for the help of the Holy Spirit, admittedly the end result is our being shown, we end up being shown one light, distilled from the two (or three) Readings. This could tempt us to think that after the active phase, we need do little other than pray. All to the contrary in fact, and what I am trying to underline here is that in this receptive phase, during the descent of Jesus' light, two stages are involved: one which leads to *one general light* and the second to *one clear distinct expression of Jesus' will*. What we need to understand is that each of these two receptive stages requires an effort. True, they are two different efforts, but still, they are efforts.

The first stage, which is the one that leads to *one general light* consists in the reading and re-reading effort of the texts, reading while praying and begging. It requires going back and forth from one text to the other: it requires a renewed commitment to the Lord.

The second stage, which is the main subject of this article, takes us from the *one general light* received to *a clear, distinct, light*, expressing Jesus' will. This second stage of the receptive phase is also characterised by an effort, a form of wrestling with the Lord, similar to the wrestling of Jacob with the Angel in the book of Genesis 32:24-30.

"So Jacob was left all alone, and there a man wrestled with him until daybreak. When the man saw that he could not overpower Jacob, he struck the socket of Jacob's hip and dislocated it as they wrestled. Then the man said, "Let me go, for it is daybreak." But Jacob replied, "I will not let you go unless you bless me." "What is your name?" the man asked. "Jacob," he replied. Then the man said, "Your name will no longer be Jacob, but Israel, because you have struggled with God and with men, and you have prevailed." And Jacob requested, "Please tell me your name." But he replied, "Why do you ask my name?" Then he

blessed Jacob there. So Jacob named the place Peniel, saying, "Indeed, I have seen God face to face, and yet my life was spared."

Having received Jesus' light, then, since it is not yet clear, we need to wrestle with Him until He clarifies what He meant with the general light. Yes, receiving the general light is definitely a solid criterium of discernment, indicating the Holy Spirit's action in us. In the book on *Lectio* I admit to a degree of audacity in saying with 95% of certainty that it is Jesus who is starting to communicate with us and that it is not our own thoughts that we are hearing, the reason being that the two texts are saying the same thing. I consider this as a major criterium of discernment. However, having the one general light does not indicate that the process of listening has come to an end. And this is my point in the present book. We need to be careful and not stop *Lectio* at this stage. Not only that, but we have to bear in mind that there is a degree of serious wrestling which needs to take place in order to have this light become clear. Yes the supernatural light of the Holy Spirit has been given, but it has not completed its entire journey by reaching the edge of the will and revealing the act to be performed.

Indeed, now it is necessary to gird our loins once more, separate ourselves from any human attachment we may have, offering it to Jesus and placing our will totally into His Hands. To reiterate, we might be tempted to stop *Lectio* on receipt of the supernatural light. But we need to renew our wrestling with the Holy Spirit. This is why Jacob is wrestling with the Angel (the Angel here represents God himself). *Lectio* gives the impression of seeming to end here: *"Let me go, for it is daybreak."* But we should not surrender after such a feeling for *Lectio* has definitely not finished: *"But Jacob replied, "I will not let you go unless you bless me.""* This is the attitude to have while we are at this stage of *Lectio*. We need the blessing of the clear light, otherwise... we truncate *Lectio* and remain in the dark about how to put the light into action.

There is something deep and sacred about "wrestling" with God. The Angel here in this passage represents God, Jesus. Why do we need to wrestle with Him? The answer is the same: He wants to befriend us and to friends he says everything. Most significantly and poignantly, however, He does not impose himself or force himself on us. He initially waits for our first prayer and demand and gives us his general light. Then since what is at stake is sacred (the incarnation of this light in us, with a total collaboration of our mind and will), and because we are called to renew this likeness with God which we have lost, we are invited to make a greater commitment, to offer our will to Jesus, putting it into his hands, and to insist repeatedly: "what does this light mean in practice, how and where does it touch my will?" Thereby we renew our determination in a more radical way, unconditionally, and wait for His reply. It is imperative that we don't let him go before He clarifies what He has meant by this general light as to how it can become incarnate in us.

As a conclusion and learning from Scripture, we can say that this second phase of the descent of the light is embodied in this "wrestling" and "prevailing": *"you have struggled with God and with men, and you have prevailed". Lectio* in the final analysis embodies wrestling with God - and prevailing! What a mystery! God wanting to be conquered by us!

Understanding with St. Augustine

"Crede Ut Intelligas"

St. Augustine reflected deeply on the relationship between on the one hand the act of believing in the Word of God and on the other the search for understanding with our mind. St. Augustine always honoured the mind and sought after understanding our faith. He summarises our first effort in twofold pieces of advice: "Crede Ut Intelligas". Let us see what the two steps which he suggests reveal.

First St. Augustine invites us to believe in the Word of God: "Crede". He places the act of believing in the Word in first place. This consists of our initial effort and prayer: "give me O Lord your Holy Spirit and show me your will."

What is not so apparent in St. Augustine's advice is that, as a response, God starts by giving us his general light. God's reply is necessary, however, and is the starting point of the second stage "Ut Intelligas".

This is where we need to understand St. Augustine's next step given to us more indirectly: let this light God has given us fertilise our mind, let it illumine our mind, let it interact with our mind, seeking greater understanding: Lord explain what you mean by this light.

St. Augustine constantly sought understanding the contents of our faith. But it is not always properly underlined that to do so, he is placing himself under the light his act of faith has already obtained. He wants to understand, he knows he has the right to understand; he knows that this is part of being Christian, that God honours our mind, that God wants to illumine our mind; that God wants to make real friends of us, that He wants to explain from within.

This step of understanding the general light given to us by our initial act of faith is a very important stage. And making it with the right intention is paramount for its success. What is the "right intention"? It is to obey God, to obey His Word. To achieve this, we need clarity: we need to involve our mind totally, until the light reaches the edge of our will, showing us how it can change our will.

As we see, St. Augustine summarises the whole process in this phrase: "Crede ut intelligat". "believe in order to understand".

Summing it up then: we need to realise that the process according to St. Augustine also has two stages as does the one outlined above: 1- to believe, seeking God's will. As a result, we have a light, a general light. 2- to understand this light now and see how it applies to our life: "intelligat". This is the second phase we address in this article, where we seek, wrestling, offering our entire mind and will, to let this light descend and fertilise our mind and thus becoming clear. In this way we become the Lord's true friends because "He explains everything to us" with clarity (John 15:15) - He explains what He wills for us. Our question: "what does it mean in practice?" obtains an answer: the same

37

light becomes clear, "ut intelligat" – an "intelligent understanding" is realised.

Quotes From St. Augustine

"Our faith is not a blind adherence but a journey into the depths of divine truth. Therefore, it is necessary to cultivate a deeper comprehension of the faith we profess." (Sermon 117, 8)

"The more we know of God, the more our faith is enriched. Thus, seeking an intelligent grasp of our beliefs is not a mere intellectual exercise but a means to grow closer to the divine truth." (*Confessions*, Book 10, Chapter 23)

"It is the duty of every Christian to seek an intelligent understanding of their faith, for in doing so, they will come to appreciate the profound wisdom of God's plan." (*City of God*, Book 19, Chapter 23)

Of course, the quotes above could be erroneously understood in a wrong way, that is, as if understanding faith is the goal of our life, or as if we are saved by this understanding (Gnosticism). The goal of our Christian life is to seek God's will and to put it into practice. Hence the correct context to understand St. Augustine's advice and quotes is *Lectio Divina*.

The Three Graces of St. Teresa

When St. Teresa of Avila explains spiritual life, she mentions something which is in the province of Theology. She says that the grace itself is one thing and to understand it quite another, and that yet another is to transmit it or explain it to others: "it is one favour that the Lord should grant this favour; but quite another to understand what favour and what grace it is; and still another to be able to describe and explain it" (*Life* 17,5. See also 12,6; 23,11 and 30,4)[5]

---

[5] St. Thomas Aquinas discusses two of the three graces in the *Summa Theologica*, Part I-II, Question 110, Article 1. Francisco de Osuna also mentions two of these graces in his *Third Abecedary*, chapter 2.

These three graces are often presented as two categories of graces: the first one, being the grace itself, which is considered to be of a particular category (sanctifying grace) and the second and the third are extra graces, not necessarily considered as sanctifying grace. They are considered to be freely given for the growth of the mystical body of Jesus.

One needs to remember also that the grace itself cannot, by definition, be felt. While the second and third graces can be felt: one cannot have an understanding of the grace without a clear awareness of it. One cannot receive help from God to explain and transmit what has been understood without the help of a grace which penetrates our conscious mind.

Traditionally, the second and the third graces are considered as not the grace itself, and therefore can be reserved for some people only, not necessarily for sanctification[6]. They are graces given for the ministry. But this view weakens our proper understanding of the second and third graces for the believer and fails to show the connection between the first grace and the other two. Consequently one misses an important aspect of the mission of the faithful: to witness to Christ, and to have a well-developed relationship with Him, and that helped by this friendship He wants to establish with us where He explains everything to us, as He says in St. John (John 15:15)

In my humble view, we are missing something very important related to our spiritual growth, to our mission in life, and to our *Lectio Divina*, if we ignore this connection. In fact, the second and third graces enhance the normal growth and development of the main grace in us, going from the supraconscious (above consciousness) communication of the main grace to the conscious part, or if you will, from the general light to the precise light.

In this sense I would say that in the case of *Lectio Divina* the first grace (the grace itself) is the *general light* given to us, and that the second and third graces (understanding and putting into practice) constitute the

---

[6] See *Summa Theologica*, Part I-II, Question 110.

descent of the first grace into the conscious part of our mind and will: the clear light. In this sense the second and third graces are not optional as one would think, or just given to some for the ministry and the growth of Jesus' mystical body - on the contrary they are integral to the process of Jesus' communication with us. The three graces are in fact one grace, one process of descent in three stages.

The Motorcade

The image of the motorcade can help us understand the effort of facilitating the descent of the light until it reaches our will. When an important political personality is travelling, sometimes we have two sets of motorcycles opening the way for him or her. Similarly, we, like the important personality, are not the Light, and we do not direct the light. Our role is to simply open the way for it to descend closer to out will that needs to be healed. Thus we humble ourselves, we beg and ask, being more attentive to Jesus' whispering (remember Elijah's gentle breeze), telling us what He wants to change in us. This entails another effort of being humble and begging to allow what is now already supernatural but too general, too abstract, to become precise, clear, and practical. Only when the light has reached our will, to indicate first and foremost a practical area that needs changing in our heart, may we then consider that fruition is in sight.

The Narrow Way

We all know that when it comes to listening to the Lord, we all struggle so that we spontaneously ask: "Lord, will only a few people be saved?" In other words: "Will only a few people be able to Listen to you?" In reply the Lord will say: "Strive to enter through the narrow gate...." (Luke 13:24) "Small is the gate and narrow the way that leads to Life and only a few find it." (Matthew 7:14)
What, then, is the "narrow gate" and what is the "narrow way"? These two images sum up to what lengths we should go to completely humble ourselves. The degree to which we should humble ourselves is encapsulated in the words: The last will be first, and the first will be last.

"Matthew 20:16) "Take the lowest place." (Luke 14:10) "Humble yourself". (James 410, 1P 310) The choice, then, is to meet the Lord either in the "middle" of our mind, or at the "bottom" of it. The "middle" of our mind means keeping distant from our will, from the core of our being, from real change, in the high abstract regions of the mind, and not allowing God to reach our core. Meeting Him at the "middle" offers us a general and abstract light / understanding of the will of God. However, if we allow Jesus' light to reach the "bottom" of our Mind, at the junction with our Will, the light He will shed on us is more concrete, more incarnate, for it will generate an inner action in the Will. Sadly we sometimes settle for meeting the Lord at the "top" of our mind, and this fails to bear fruit. This is why the typical effort required of *Lectio Divina*, the typical effort of "listening" is to go down, to bow down, to humble ourselves, to descend into ourselves, opening the way within us for the Word of God, so it can reach our will and illumine it, heal it, transform it, sanctify it. There is a deep desire in Jesus for his Word to enter within us, but He never forces us. This is the reason for his asking us to open the narrow door of our inner world and to make in ourselves an entry way for Him - that is, the narrow way.

The space we dig out for Christ in ourselves has: Height, Depth, Width, Length. (see Ephesians 3:18)

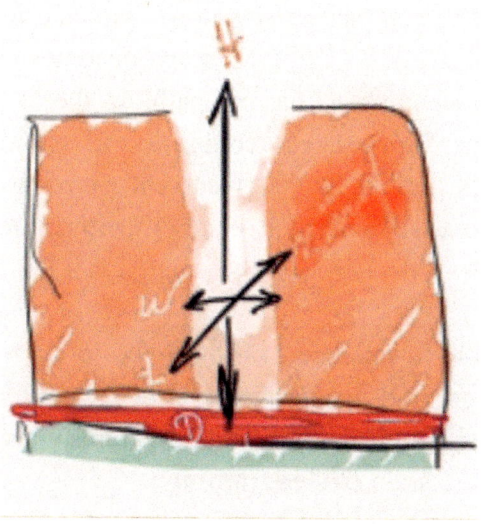

It is vital to humble ourselves in:
• Height: for the Word comes from Him who is higher than heaven, connecting the soil of our being with the Divine.
• Depth: the Word we receive has to come down and reach the intersection between our mind and will, touching the will to show it what to do.
• Width: the Word cannot carry/bear in our heart any other idol / "god" with it. No competitors, no worries.
• Length: our commitment to the Word is for ever.

1- Opening the door of our inner being to Jesus' Word, is the most challenging preparation we can make to receive Him. Remember the first type of soil in the parable of the Sower being totally closed to the Word of God.

2- Digging a narrow path deep and humbly within ourselves, so deep, as to expose our naked will to the light of Jesus, allowing the Word to reach it, are the only ways to receive God's Word within us and be transformed by His Holy Spirit. Indeed, in order for *Lectio Divina* to succeed, we first need – by the Grace of God and by our resilient efforts – to become able, in a personal encounter with the Word of God, to listen to His Voice. This personal encounter, consequently, necessitates:

1- Our opening we open the "narrow door" and entering through it.
2- Listening attentively until the Message becomes clear by touching our will, thereby opening a "narrow path" to the Word in us as it is passing through us: "Someone asked him, "Lord, will only a few people be saved?" He answered them, "Strive to enter through the narrow gate, for many, I tell you, will attempt to enter but will not be strong enough." (Luke 322-30)

Will many be able to practise *Lectio Divina* in a fruitful way? Since *Lectio Divina* is so vital for our Spiritual Life, "only a few people will be saved" can easily and rightly be translated this way: "only a few will be able to practise *Lectio Divina* fruitfully.."

Conclusion

As a conclusion, therefore, when we practise *Lectio Divina*, and when we start to sense that the supernatural light of God is starting to appear, occurring when the two texts say the same thing, it is important not only to rejoice with gratitude, but to continue to open the way, humbling ourselves more and more, asking the Lord to tell us how He wants to incarnate the word or light or indication He is revealing to us. Only humbling ourselves will open the way for Jesus' Word to reach us, touch our will, heal us, challenge us, enflame us. Within reason, therefore, we should not stop *Lectio* until the grace of God has touched us.

II- From Pharisee to Publican

One of the most difficult things in Spiritual Life is to explain what we are supposed to do in order to make *Lectio Divina* work.

In fact, often *Lectio Divina* fails to work, not because God or Jesus does not want to speak to us, or the Holy Spirit does not want to work in us! On the contrary, Jesus longs to speak to us with every fibre of his being. Unfortunately what we fail to understand is: to which exact extent our efforts encourage this, as well as, how we are supposed to facilitate a successful result in *Lectio* in order to make *Lectio* work.

St. Teresa of Avila puts it in a nutshell: not knowing the difference in the way the Grace of God works between the general help and the particular help He gives us, makes our spiritual life lukewarm, makes *Lectio Divina* "abort" quite often. We are often lost between two extremes and cannot find the right measure in between. The extremes are either to be really aggressive, overriding the grace of God and His freedom, to act in fact with an arrogantly, or, to be too passive and fail to do what we are supposed to do! So, in the end, the Grace of God, or more precisely the personal and direct action of the Holy Spirit, does not occur.

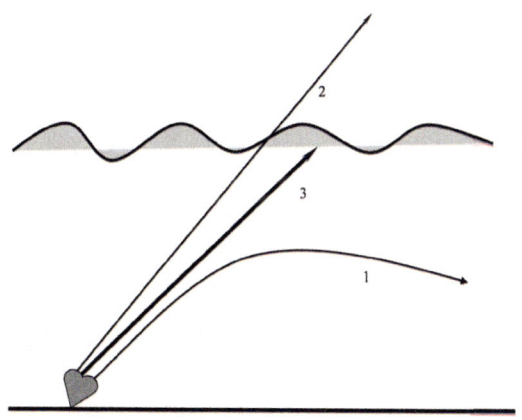

If we look at the drawing above, which shows our heart, immersed in the waters of our being, about to give itself to God, and also showing the surface of the water which is the limit between God's freedom and ours, we will see illustrated three different ways to offer ourselves to Him, three ways of interacting with God.

It is not uncommon for people to get the general light of God, which corresponds to the moment where the two or more texts are saying the same thing, although through different words, and in different places in the texts. But the part of the journey that is paradoxically more difficult occurs, when crossing from this moment to the moment when a clear light causes us to really hear what Jesus wants from us. Why is this so?

One of the reasons is that the person, after having received the general light of the Word of God, switches to almost a more receptive mode, where most of the attention resembles a ruminating state, where the person is almost in a dreamlike state repeating the words that speak to him in each text, while expecting the clear will of Jesus to pop up at a certain point, out of His pure grace.

The reality, by contrast, is that there is still an important part of the journey of the descent of the word of God in us that is as yet unfinished, that is, proceeding from (a) to (b)).

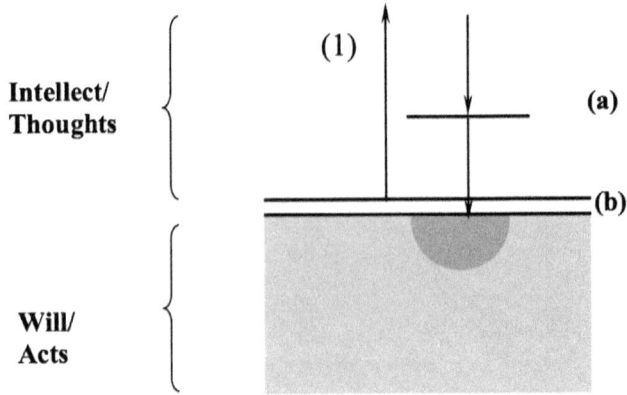

How do we go from (a) to (b)? From the general supernatural light to the particular supernatural light? From understanding that the Lord is talking about Mercy, for instance, as a general reality of the Gospel, to understanding that He is asking me to reconcile with a specific person?

Should I just continue to re-read the parts of the texts that now talk to me and wait until Jesus clarifies His request? It is most probable that nothing will happen because if this is done (i.e. switching to a more receptive attitude) we stop our collaboration with the Lord, stop showing our will.

It is as if the Lord has been denied even a modicum of encouragement to dare enter more deeply within our being and point out the area He wants to heal. *Lectio Divina* – like any serious prayer – is an interaction between two beings, God, and us, where each has his free will and is supposed to use it. If one stops showing his will and desire, it blocks the process! It is as if two persons were supposed to shake hands and one extended his hand to the mid-distance between them and the other, after having started to extend his hand, withdrew it before reaching the mid-distance. The two hands will not meet, and in our case they will not continue to work together – it is as if one person has ceased to collaborate!

The Lord will not continue to enter within us, because we are not allowing Him to do so! We are receptive, but this receptivity is passive and seems to have given up using his own will. It is as if somebody went to see the doctor saying that he is wounded and happened to stop in the middle of the process of taking off his clothes to show the wound! How would the doctor then see the wound and apply the appropriate medicine to it? Will the doctor apply force and he himself remove the patient's clothes? Not really! He will respect the reluctance of the patient to go further! This is in fact what is really happening! We stop in the middle of the process, ironically thinking that by becoming more "receptive" we are really doing the right thing!

On the contrary, the desire and the intensity of the begging should increase! We should not simply latch onto the word of God (say, Mercy) and apply it to our own way of thinking, but instead direct our humble requests, face to face with the Word of God, to the correct area, namely, towards our will which is sick – in the direction of incarnation of that will.

Digging Deeper

It is by digging deeper within ourselves that we can open the way in us for the Word of God to descend, to continue its journey until it reaches the juncture between the mind and the will! The end-product, so to speak, of *Lectio* is that the word of God is supposed to point out to a certain area in our will what needs to be healed, changed and transformed on a particular day.

The temptation, however, is to unconsciously take a more spiritually comfortable attitude that will jeopardise the continuation of the descent of the Word of God in us toward our will.

Jesus himself said to the Pharisees: *"It is not the healthy who need a doctor, but the sick"* (Luke 5:31, Matthew 9:12; Mark 2:17). He warned the Pharisees by saying: those who think they are doing well, have no need of Him. And herein lies the crux of the matter that the practice of *Lectio Divina* reminds each one of us of on a daily basis: are you spiritually healthy? Are you doing well? Are you ill? Are you blind? Often our attitude, or if you prefer the spirit in which we practise *Lectio Divina*, seems to say that yes, we are fine. This is the big risk we run when we practise *Lectio Divina* in a rather half-hearted way.

By faith, out of the mysterious and deep light of faith, we know that since God is God, pure, holy, immense, there must be in us (compared to Him) some dark area, some wounds that need healing, some things that need change. But they are yet to come to light! While we have this general light telling us that the will of God for us today for instance is

"Mercy", we fail to see how it applies in us! Jesus will not force himself on us, showing us what He wants to change! Faith tells us that some area in us needs healing and needs to learn mercy, needs to soften and be more forgiving, and welcoming, but we cannot understand how it is supposed to happen and towards whom! Faith, true faith, tells us that we are blind; faith, true faith is pushing us in a renewed way today, out of our comfort zone, telling us that we are not fine, that we need Jesus!

We need to shift our attitude, from an attitude of sufficiency, to an attitude of need, dependency, and indigence. We must accept true vulnerability, the need for divine help and true change.

We can humble ourselves by switching our attitude from the Pharisee's attitude (one who feels he is really fine and lacks nothing particular that can come from God), to the attitude of the Publican, who has come face to face with his true self, devoid of lies, welcoming God's light, as crude and harsh as it can be, because he knows that this is the source of possible healing. We can switch attitude, from the person who is not in need of a doctor to the person who is in urgent and vital need of a doctor and for healing, from the self-satisfied Pharisee to the spiritually poor Publican who counts on God's mercy.

Remember: who begged for his life? The blind man in the Gospel. It was vital for him!

When I continue my *Lectio Divina*, what should my attitude be? Am I to focus on my healer, Jesus, or I am just to relax and spend some quality time with God? Am I dealing with the text, trying to unravel some message that is only for me, or am I hardly able to bear my state and am asking for the mercy of God, for his healing and to show me my real illness!

Once the blind mean sees, he sees his own defects, his own lack, the space in him for Jesus.

Faith tells me that despite all the progress I might have made, I am still in need of starting today anew, and that I am a really blind person, a really ill person in need of Jesus!

This is the real question *Lectio Divina* urges me to ask every day: am I in need of Jesus today or are we just nice buddies? Or a comfortable worshipper? Or just a scrupulous member of the faith who has to fulfil some sort of prayer routine just to feel that all is well?

The general help of the grace of God provides us with a switch every day, empowering us to turn from the attitude of the Pharisee to that of the Publican.

"To some who were confident of their own righteousness and looked down on everyone else, Jesus told this parable: "Two men went up to the temple to pray, one a Pharisee and the other a tax collector. The Pharisee stood by himself and prayed: 'God, I thank you that I am not like other people—robbers, evildoers, adulterers—or even like this tax collector. I fast twice a week and give a tenth of all I get.' "But the tax collector stood at a distance. He would not even look up to heaven, but beat his breast and said, 'God, have mercy on me, a sinner.' "I tell you that this man, rather than the other, went home justified before God. For all those who exalt themselves will be humbled, and those who humble themselves will be exalted." (Luke 18:9-14)

Humbling oneself is really in the hands of each human being! It is at the heart of the art of spiritual life. We all need to learn this art:

"many who are first will be last, and many who are last will be first" (Mathew 19:30; 20:16)

Humble yourself before God and He will fill your heart. It is in your hands, within your capability, it is your decision! Every day gathering together all our dispersed energy, pushing yourself out of your comfort zone, this is within your capability, within your means.

Lord Jesus, show us the way to truly humble ourselves. Our Lady, help us and show us how we should even beg more once we start to see the supernatural light of God; open the way in us for the Word of God, to beg our Doctor to show us our wound by opening all our being without any condition or restriction. Show us O Mary, the journey into ourselves, the journey of descent, humbling ourselves, creating a greater space within ourselves for Jesus' vital healing! Show us Our Lady how to renew it every day.

Remember, there are many passages in the Scriptures which give us the indication of the necessity to humble ourselves in order to receive the Grace of God, that is, the particular help of the Grace of God, which is the personal and direct intervention of the Holy Spirit in us:

"Humble yourselves, therefore, under God's mighty hand, that he may lift you up in due time." (1 Peter 5:6)

"For whoever exalts himself will be humbled, and whoever humbles himself will be exalted" (Matthew 23:12 and see Luke 14:11).

"He has brought down rulers from their thrones, but has exalted the humble." (Luke 1:52)

"Humble yourselves before the Lord, and He will exalt you." (James 4:10)

"But He gives us more grace. This is why it says: "God opposes the proud, but gives grace to the humble."" (James 4:6)

"This is what the Lord GOD says: 'Remove the turban, and take off the crown. Things will not remain as they are: Exalt the lowly and bring low the exalted." (Ez 21:26)

"You do not delight in sacrifice, or I would bring it; you do not take pleasure in burnt offerings. My sacrifice, O God, is a broken spirit; a broken and contrite heart you, God, will not despise." (Ps 51:16-17)

III- *Lectio Divina*'s Act of Humility

The Light Shed by the Canaanite Woman

Introduction

The most difficult part of *Lectio Divina* is to know what action depends on us and then how to implement it. It, in fact, covers the first request we make when we say: « Lord, tell me what you want from me? », and then hearing the answer.

Asking depends on us and seems harsh, difficult even arduous. What, however, is the relationship between asking and receiving an answer? Is there a way of asking? Is there a degree of intensity needed? By implementing certain conditions, can we really trigger Jesus' answer? Are we putting an unneeded pressure on Him, forcing Him to respond, or are we ourselves supposed to create this pressure? In the main book on *Lectio Divina* ("*Lectio Divina* at the School of Mary") it is said that this pressure is not only necessary but that there is a reason: it does not annoy the Lord, but instead it creates a needed space in us for the reception of his Word.

Two drawings have been used to illustrate what we are supposed to do in order to receive the word, and to show the intensity of the begging. The first one appears in the main book mentioned above and the second in an article on the website.

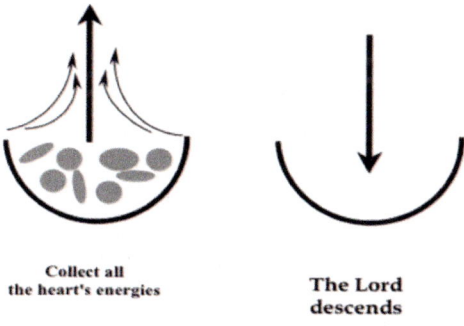

**Collect all
the heart's energies**

**The Lord
descends**

The needed purity that allows us to receive the Word of God has also been underlined and explained. Purity is the condition of receiving the Word of God, the condition of being heard by the Lord. "Blessed the pure of heart, for they will see God" (Matthew 5). Purity is to put Him and His healing Word in first place in our life. It is to consider Him really in our heart as our real and only God! A sincere heart knows how many other gods live in us! This is why, every day, by putting Him above everything else in our heart, above any other god, we perform a renewed act of purity that attracts the Word of the Lord to us. This act of purity, or humility or of humbling ourselves, or begging (it is all one), attracts the Lord to our heart, whereby we create a real pure space for Him. Nothing is done once and for all time, however, which is why, every day, for a new Word to be received, we must renew this act of purity. This act costs us everything, again, every day. God is God, and He should be treated as God. *Lectio* is not an intellectual game or a fun toy to use every day. It is serious, and it deals with serious matters: our transformation! Nothing else matters in our day! Progress, spiritual growth, managed by Jesus Himself is fundamental.

General Help and Particular Help of the Grace of God

Like any other virtue humility has two aspects. One depends on us and the other one on God. Here we will be addressing the acts of humility that depend on us. It is worth adding that to say "depend on us" never means not to be counting on the Grace of God. In fact, Faith and

Theology teach us that the general help of the Grace of God precedes our action always. And any good we can do starts always from God. What "depends on us" can only be done by leaning on the "General help of the Grace of God" which is always given to us. Becoming aware of the pre-existence of this type of Grace of God given to us, then, is fundamental, because we need to avail ourselves of it. Thus, simply knowing that it is given to us should result in the natural reaction of implementing it. Since it is given to us and is constantly available, if we do not use it the grace will be lost. As we will see below, more importantly we will miss the opportunity of obtaining the "specific help of the grace of God".

Here we would like to address a section of the science of the "general help of the grace of God" and its use. How to use the "general help", and to which extent. What is at stake with the "general help" and what is its relationship with the "particular help of the grace of God"? In fact, there is a vital relationship between them: the first leads to the second and is a condition for triggering the second. Therefore, not having full personal and practical clarity for each of the faithful concerning the general help (and its relationships with the "particular help"), inflicts great loss in the spiritual life as St. Teresa of Avila underlines in her Autobiography, Chapter 14 paragraph 6 (see below).

It is true that for some the use of the "general help" and "particular help" could be seen as restricted to practise of the Prayer of the Heart only. This is not the case; in fact the entire practical implementation of the Grace of God is governed by them. As a consequence, their functioning and mechanism is present in each and every spiritual act that puts the human being in direct contact with God, *Lectio Divina* being part of these spiritual acts. Whoever practises it needs to understand with incisive clarity this teaching about the relationship between the two types of help of the grace of God. This is what we will try to show.

In her writings, St. Teresa of Avila mentions the "General help" and the "Particular help" of the Grace of God: "For many purposes it is necessary to be learned; and it would be very useful to have some learning here, in order to explain what is meant by general or particular help (for there are many who do not know this) and how it is now the Lord's will that the soul should see this particular help (as they say) with its own eyes; and learning would also serve to explain many other things about which mistakes may be made." (*Life*14,6; see Third Mansions 1,2 as well; Fifth Mansions 2,3)

She will then explain that in order to practise the "prayer of recollection" we need to use the "general help" of the Grace of God that is constantly being given to us. And that in the "Prayer of Quiet", we receive the "particular help" of the Grace of God that is supernatural (Fourth Mansions 1,1), that is, infused. Of course, St. Teresa of Avila's explanations are essentially given for the practice of the Prayer of the Heart. However, we need to see how they apply to *Lectio Divina*.

These notions of general and particular help of the grace of God belong to the Theology of Grace that one covers while doing the basic four years of Theology. For instance, St. Thomas Aquinas, in his *Summa Theologica*, I-II Q.109 a. 6, addresses this issue. He mentions two needs: one is the main need, which is to receive the Grace of God. For *Lectio Divina* it will be listening and understanding the Word that Jesus gives us every day; this can only happen with the direct and personal intervention of the Holy Spirit. Remember that *Lectio Divina* is like a small Annunciation. And that in order to have the incarnation of the Word in Mary (and a word in us) She needed the direct and personal intervention of the Holy Spirit: "how will this happen?" She asks. The angel explains: "the Holy Spirit…"

St. Thomas continues: "and the second [need] precedes it: to prepare ourselves to receive this first and main Grace". We need this second grace in order to receive the first and main grace. Since the grace that prepares us leads us to the main Grace, "knowing the existence of this preparative grace, and learning how to use it" are decisive and vital for all our spiritual life, worship and Christian life.

This preparative grace is the "general help of the Grace of God" that we use in the Prayer of Recollection, to get closer to God, offering ourselves to Him, putting ourselves into the Hands of God. For whoever is acquainted with the diagrams of the Prayer of the Heart (see book "Praying with the Heart: The Little Way to Jesus" by Jean Khoury), the general help of the Grace of God is used by us to move in the water, so to speak, from the bottom of the sea to the surface, offering ourselves to Jesus/Mary. To use a more common teaching from the Gospel, it is this general common grace given to us that helps us "ask", "knock", "seek"... the Holy Spirit, a Word from God...as Jesus invites us to do.

In the Prayer of the Heart, the "main" grace mentioned by St. Thomas Aquinas, that is, the particular help of the grace of God, is when Jesus comes, takes us and places us within Him: this is the main action of the Holy Spirit that puts us in a direct and personal relationship with the Risen Lord.

St. Thomas Aquinas' article is meant to answer this question: "Whether a man, by himself and without the external aid of grace, can prepare himself for Grace?" (*Summa Theologica*, I-II Q.109 a. 6) Let us examine St. Thomas' answer in detail: he begins, "I answer that, the preparation of the human will for good is twofold" He will then explain the existence of two types of graces. One is the main grace we need, i.e. the intervention of the Holy Spirit in us and the other one prepares us to receive the main grace.

1- The main Grace, the infused one: this is the one we need and await in order to "enter in God" (merit eternal life). This is the particular help of the Grace of God that places us within Him.

2- and the other grace is the one that prepares us for it, that leads us to it, that helps our free will to choose God, go toward Him in order to receive his grace. This is the "general help of the Grace of God", that leads us to the "border" or "meeting point", that "prepares us", makes us ready to receive the Main grace.

As one can see, the second leads to the first one. In *Lectio Divina*, one cannot separate the "begging" effort ("Prayer") from God's answer ("Contemplation"). One is ordered to the other.

Let us now read St. Thomas' key passage where he in fact describes "Contemplation" or better said: the personal and direct intervention of the Holy Spirit: "the first [grace], whereby it is prepared to operate rightly and to enjoy God; and this preparation of the will cannot take place without the habitual gift of grace, which is the principle of meritorious works, as stated above." Without this Grace we cannot be introduced into God, drink God, "enjoy God" and "operate rightly" in Him, listen properly to the Word of God. This is the Main Grace we need from God. Now, how can we receive this grace? This is the central issue of this article. Do we need the help from God to receive the Main infused supernatural Grace?

This chapter can be said to be a key one because our spiritual life is about receiving "Grace upon Grace" (John 1), and the question is: how can we receive the Grace? How can we prepare ourselves? St. Thomas' reply is swift to enlighten us: "There is a second way in which the human will may be taken to be prepared for the gift of habitual grace itself. Now in order that man prepare himself to receive this gift, it is not necessary to presuppose any further habitual gift in the soul, otherwise we should go on to infinity. But we must presuppose a gratuitous gift of God, Who moves the soul inwardly or inspires the good wish." This is the key phrase, "a gratuitous gift of God". This gratuitous gift is constantly given, to everybody, it is the "general help of the grace of God" that St. Teresa of Avila mentions.

We can complete this with his reply to the 4th objection: "4: It is the part of man to prepare his soul, since he does this by his free-will. And yet he does not do this without the [general] help of God moving him, and drawing him to Himself, as was said above."

As we can see our part is to "prepare ourselves" in the sense of "to go inwardly" as he stated, to get closer to the meeting point where we are supposed to receive the main grace. Begging with all our heart, creating a space in us for the Word of God, performing an act of "humbling ourselves" is done by the "general help of the grace of God". This is the main arduous effort in the practice of *Lectio Divina*. It has to be done, otherwise, the direct and personal action of the Holy Spirit does not come about.

Lectio's Act of Humility

"Act of Humility" here means: the act of humbling ourselves, lowering ourselves, bowing. It is a descent into oneself that only we ourselves can bring about, a descent that depends on us. The general help of the grace of God is offered to us continuously. Consequently, during *Lectio Divina* it is imperative to use the general help of the grace of God, in order to allow Lectio to function. This part depends on us as we go about our meeting with the Lord who desires so much to talk to us.

This act of lowering ourselves, therefore, is necessary because it prepares the place that the Word will occupy. This descent, or lowering of ourselves, greatly enhances the intensity of our begging. Once the intensity crosses the red line so to speak, we can consider that we have reached the degree of preparedness of Our Lady, and in this way the Word will come to dwell in us without hesitation. This act of humility or lowering has in itself some of that "aggressiveness" or "violence" to it which the Gospel talks about. So when the Gospel says "to enter by force" into the Kingdom this in fact means to make full use of the General help of the Grace of God, to the limits of the act, where its fruitfulness is capable of seducing God, i.e. triggering the Action of the Holy Spirit, namely. *"violent people seize it* [the kingdom of God] *by force"* (Matthew 11,12) Entering the kingdom, thus, means to win the special help of the grace of God.

A very humble Carmelite Father with great experience in the spiritual life, said one day that humility had in itself some sort of aggressiveness. At first glance it is difficult to understand such a statement, for how can humility and aggressiveness be united?!

Does the Gospel mention this act of lowering oneself? Yes, many times we hear the Scriptures inviting us to lower ourselves, saying that God gives his grace to the humble (James 4:6.10, 1 Peter 5:5; Proverbs 3:34; and Mathew 23:12)! This shows that there is something within our capability and should be done. We have a choice to make, and it is in Our Lady that we can find the most wholesome example. We can also find it partially realised in different people in the Gospel.

Let us take for example the Canaanite woman and let us closely consider her persistence, this sort of stubbornness, in her request! We have the impression that nothing can stop her as she moves swiftly toward her goal: to save her daughter who is ill. She does what depends on her, and she does it to the maximum and therefore she will reach the red line mentioned above, that is, the line where we start to seduce Christ, to win Him over. In another comparable passage of the Gospel we hear praise given by Jesus to the faith of a Centurion which I think also applies perfectly to this amazing woman: "I tell you, I have not found such great faith even in Israel." (Luke 7:9) Here are the two accounts of the Canaanite.

Matthew 15:21-28	Mark 7:24-30
Leaving that place, Jesus withdrew to the region of Tyre and Sidon. 22 A Canaanite woman from that vicinity came to him, crying out, "Lord, Son of David, have mercy on me! My daughter is demon-possessed and suffering terribly."	*"Jesus left that place and went to the vicinity of Tyre. He entered a house and did not want anyone to know it; yet he could not keep his presence secret. 25 In fact, as soon as she heard about him, a woman whose little daughter was possessed by an impure spirit came and fell at his feet. 26 The woman was a Greek, born in Syrian Phoenicia. She begged Jesus to drive the demon out of her daughter.*
23 Jesus did not answer a word. So his disciples came to him and urged him, "Send her away, for she keeps crying out after us."	

24 He answered, "I was sent only to the lost sheep of Israel." 25 The woman came and knelt before him. "Lord, help me!" she said. 26 He replied, "It is not right to take the children's bread and toss it to the dogs." 27 "Yes it is, Lord," she said. "Even the dogs eat the crumbs that fall from their master's table." 28 Then Jesus said to her, "Woman, you have great faith! Your request is granted." And her daughter was healed at that moment.	27 "First let the children eat all they want," he told her, "for it is not right to take the children's bread and toss it to the dogs." 28 "Lord," she replied, "even the dogs under the table eat the children's crumbs." 29 Then he told her, "For such a reply, you may go; the demon has left your daughter." 30 She went home and found her child lying on the bed, and the demon gone."

Let us examine the stages of this arduous dialogue between this woman and the different people who surround her, for this dialogue sheds an important light on our practice of *Lectio Divina*.

1a- First, we have the spontaneous attitude of the woman: she shouts her request in the midst of the crowd to make herself heard by Jesus: "Lord, Son of David, have mercy on me! My daughter is demon-possessed and suffering terribly." Let us notice that she says: "have mercy on me" (not on my daughter)
1b- Jesus' answer: nothing.

2a- Secondly, she continues her shouting and begging, harassing the Disciples.
2b- Finally, they end up by talking about her to Christ: Heal her, *"Send her away, for she keeps crying out after us."* She certainly follows what is happening and hopes that through their intercession Jesus will finally listen. She awaits an answer from Jesus. The answer comes and is extremely harsh, severe, dry, almost insulting: *"I was sent only to the lost sheep of Israel."* She has been excluded, she is nothing in His eyes. Her cause seems to be lost. This is the end. Humanly speaking. Nobody knows that the Lord is testing her to show us the extent of her faith, to give us, through her, an amazing example.

3a- What is her reaction? Dose she drop it? Does she lose hope? No!

1- this time she herself fearlessly approaches Him!

2- she kneels in front of Jesus (lowering herself, recognising who He is) and says

1- "Lord, help me!"

3b- Does anything change here? No, Jesus, in an apparent very stubborn way reiterates his rejection of the woman: "It is not right to take the children's bread and toss it to the dogs." "dogs" - in this culture a dog in the street, an abandoned dog, is considered to be nothing! It is a great insult! Jesus is excluding her, stating that she is not Jewish, and even more, that He considers her like a dog! We who are created in the image and likeness of God, are now being compared by Jesus to animals! It is really too much! He is trying her faith! A second rejection! Will she surrender?

4a- No. She will find a way to Jesus' heart, almost quoting Him and returning his words to Him. Accordingly, she lowers herself, she humbles herself, swallows her pride and renews her demand: "Yes it is, Lord," she said. "Even the dogs eat the crumbs that fall from their master's table."

4b- She wins the Lord over. "Woman, […] Your request is granted." And her daughter was healed at that moment.

The praise given to her by Jesus should impress itself on our minds: "Woman, you have great faith!". The act of faith, or more exactly the repeated acts of faith depend on whom? On what? This is the heart of the issue. We have three obstacles opposing her request, harsh obstacles and humanly insurmountable. Strangely, she will surmount them. Let us see what she will do in order to do so.

1- First she has the noise of the crowd, not directly mentioned by the text, but easily deduced from it: she shouts, and repeats her shouts with insistence.

2- She seeks the help of the disciples, insisting, not leaving them in peace until they react. They talk to the Lord.

3- With great courage, she goes directly to the Lord. She lowers herself, and kneels or prostrates herself, recognises his greatness, his power and divinity. She is not a Jew! She humbles (humiliates) herself accepting to be treated like a dog, with her actions showing she is considering the Jews to be her masters!

As an aside here, it is worth noting that if we look closely, there is certainly room for greater psychological analysis of this complex passage.

The first obstacle can be seen as the thoughts of the crowd! What the crowd actually thinks! The second obstacle is the thoughts of the disciples! And finally, the third obstacle is an apparent thought of Christ (a fake one). These are all like layers of thoughts that Faith has to pierce! Three obstacles to cross! They are a little bit like the three first soils of the Parable of the Sower (see Matthew 13).

The most important teaching we gather from this Gospel passage, then, seems to be that in our dialogue with God we need to be aware that something very important depends on us. It applies of course when we deal with the Word of God in the Scriptures – as we do in *Lectio Divina*. There is a "violence" done to ourselves (a forcing of ourselves) that needs to be implemented in order to fulfil what depends on us. Had we been submitted to such resistance from God while doing *Lectio Divina*, being at the receiving end of total silence from God, we would have abandoned our request halfway! We would never obtain the healing! *Lectio* would never function! We need to contemplate, meditate with great seriousness on the example of this Woman in order to understand ourselves, and the different layers we often imagine. It is our heart of stone that projects an image of God that has nothing to do with who He is and is a serious hindrance to the process of listening to God during *Lectio Divina*.

We need to notice how the Canaanite women interacted with Jesus: she had a series of obstacles. At each obstacle, she had a choice to make:

either to renounce or to fight back, surmount the obstacle and win! With the general help of the grace of God given to her, she did great violence to herself various times, and each time she needed greater strength than the previous one.

She asks, and each time she uses greater humility! The paradox is that the insistence of this woman, instead of being arrogant and pretentious, becomes humbler each time! She creates in herself a greater space in order to receive the miraculous action of Christ, that is, the direct and personal action of the Holy Spirit. Thus, we can, without hesitation, say about her: *"I tell you, I have not found such great faith even in Israel."* (Luke 7:9)

Here what is certainly being discussed is faith – the act of faith – but we are addressing the quality of the Act of Faith! A powerful faith, humble, which obliterates "self" and leaves room for Christ's Action only. She knows that Jesus can do it; she knows that if He wants to do it, He has the power to do so. We know that Jesus came to heal the wounded, came to save the lost and the ones who have gone astray: *"It is not the healthy who need a doctor, but the sick."* (Matthew 9:12) But in this passage of the Gospel Jesus wants to teach us something fundamental in the Spiritual Life and in order to do so, He puts on trial the faith of this woman to teach us the lesson on how to beg for the Word of God, how to go to the deepest level of our relationship with God, and not to be content with the external layer of the Word of God and of the perceptions we have of it.

At the level of the work of the Grace of God, these repeated acts of faith, this insistence, are of such "violence" and "aggressiveness" that we are stunned! The woman is of such humility, always going deeper and greater. By her insistence in trying to obtain the Grace, she is in fact creating in herself the space in order to receive the Grace. This depends on her because the general help of the grace of God is being given all the time to all of us. This is the reason why we have this passage and this Gospel lesson. Here we have a great lesson in needing to know what depends on us, in needing to know the Lord in truth, to know what He wants to give us! And we need to prepare ourselves, with "violence" in order to receive Him. He has taught us how to ask for our "daily bread" (his Word), but the quality of the demand depends on us. Totally. In a way the outcome of *Lectio Divina* depends on us in the majority of the cases. In sum, the great secret in our dealings with God is to know and work upon this knowledge that the "general help of the Grace of God" is given to us all the time! It depends on us to learn how to use it and not to hesitate to use it to the full in order to bear fruit.

Word Against Word; Thought Against All Thought

Faith is a thought, a word upon which we lean in order to go to its object, that is, the contents meant by the word. In the beginning of the account of the Canaanite woman, we have the thoughts of the Crowd (even if the crowd is only implicit in the text). Then we have the thoughts of the disciples. Finally, we have Christ's thoughts (divided into two categories: what we think they are, and what they truly are). The repeated acts of faith of the woman cross and pierce these layers of thought and each time go beyond them.

In fact, we can say that in order to make these acts of faith we have thought against thought. A real battle! One word against another. This is how our faith is guided: the thoughts that are leading it, that offer it content.

Isn't this what we do when we practise *Lectio Divina*? At each stage of it we fight thoughts that are contrary to true Faith. And in these battles, we are invited to offer a stronger thought, like a counter-offensive. Thus, we read the Sacred Texts of the two readings, and re-read them. At each level of reading we are faced with thoughts, we ripen these thoughts, a form of word from God but not yet the right one. Either we surrender, or we counter-attack, and win! It is a battle of words, of levels of depth of words! And we are searching for the True Word, the precious Pearl, and not just apparent words which are trying to convince us, selling us

65

their thoughts or their merchandise. It is like an arm-wrestling tournament! Who will win?

Indubitably *Lectio* is a battle camp and we need to go on the attack, to fight, ready to give our life for it. Dying to ourselves! Letting our ego die. Remember the Canaanite woman? She swallowed her ego!

Yes, faith is a thought that is deep, and it is fighting with thoughts that are less deep! To fight is a choice! We can easily see now how Faith contains some aggressiveness: acrimony – the conviction that one needs to win – pugnacity, combativeness, harshness. We cannot, however, outdo God in generosity.

During *Lectio* there are different types and levels of "reading" the same texts, and yet we are constantly dealing with the same texts! We re-read them relentlessly, as if we are expecting them to deliver new and mysterious sap to us! However, there are different levels of reading! There is reading and reading! We is a reading which looks to understand objectively what the text says in itself. There is another reading after it where we focus more and are healed, asking the Lord to tell us what He wants from us. There is a reading that insists with stubbornness until it reaches the spiritual level (beyond the bark or the skin of the text), namely, when the two texts "speak" and consequently say the same thing, because it is the Spirit who speaks and not the letter (*"the letter kills but the Spirit gives life"* (2 Corinthians 3:6) *"But whenever anyone turns to the Lord [whenever anyone believes], the veil is taken away."* (2 Corinthians 3:16)) And finally, we have the final prostration where we insist on obtaining the clear light about ourselves and what we want to change – from being general the light becomes clear!

Lectio Divina is a series of battles one after the other and this last one makes us win the war! Whoever does not want to undergo these battles of Faith, cannot obtain the Victory. The latter is obtained by the tip of the sword of Truth (see Ephesians 6,17). We start *Lectio* with false or superficial opinions on Faith, we aim and search for the Truth about ourselves and we do not stop until we reach it.

True Humility is Truth (see St. Teresa of Avila)!

True humility, then can be seen as the effort of preparing to receive the truth. It is an effort of descent into ourselves, digging a new space in ourselves for the Word. At the same time, it is an effort of entering into the text in-depth, going beyond the outer layer or skin of the text until we reach the juicy fruit, the Living Word who speaks through the Spirit.

Humility is to cross the false screens, the obstacles, in order to reach the heart of Truth. This too is the Act of Faith!

If we glance back at the classic anthropological diagram describing the descent of the Word in our mind, we will notice the extremes of our mind: the upper more abstract part of it (the upper arrow) and the lower one, more concrete, touching our will almost (the lower arrow).

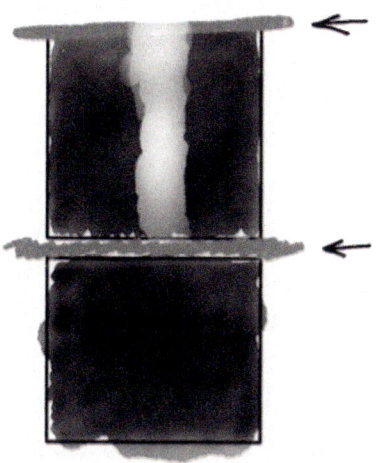

Between the two there is a journey of the descent of Christ's Word into our mind. The issue, then, is its manifestation from a general light to a particular light that points toward our will, that invites us to make an act. We can consider that this journey of descent does not happen in one fell swoop! It is a journey full of obstacles to overcome, as we have just seen above with the Canaanite woman. The warfare in which the Canaanite woman engages embodies the *Lectio Divina* warfare where Christ's Word wants to give itself, to descend into us! The Word does not descend automatically just because we have opened up the two texts of the day! On the contrary, the Word hides inside the texts waiting for us to create a space for it within us, waiting for us to go from one battle to the following until we reach it! One has to sell everything every day in order to buy the Pearl of great price (see Matthew 13:46)! It is by bowing deeply and without restraint that one can hear the Word. God hides! And we need to seek Him out! The Word of God is jealous, like the wisdom of God in the Old Testament books of wisdom, and it does not offer itself to the first comer. Only to the ones who ask for her with purity can find her!

We should now consider that the Canaanite woman is one who teaches us how to go from one stage to the next in our reading of the text! Levels of depths in the same texts! There should be no searching for quantity in the Sacred text but a looking for new depth that the Spirit only can reveal.

As we have said above, while practising *Lectio Divina* we find the suggestion that we "read" repeated four times. Each form of reading is different from the previous one:

To read in order to understand what the text says objectively.
To read in order to search for Christ's will.
To read in order to find a word / a sentence unique to both texts.
To reach in order to find the practical point that Christ want us to act upon.
To cross from one level to the other of these efforts of reading, going into greater depth, we should imitate the Canaanite woman: we should set ourselves the goal of going deeper into ourselves, in order for Christ to reveal to us this part of Truth; of healing; this new act that He offers us and suggests we put into practice.

The Other Aspect of Humility

In the following quotation St. James is asking us to receive the Word of God with humility (or meekness or gentleness,, depending on the translation): *"humbly accept the word planted in you, which can save you"* (James 1,21).

Some might use this quote to counter what has been said about the "violence" one needs to use in the begging process of *Lectio Divina*. Others might say: ok, violence on one hand and humility or meekness on the other hand, how can we combine both?

The answer could be enlarged in two points at least:

1- Understanding who talks to us during *Lectio Divina*.
2- Crossing from the necessary begging to the gentle reception of the Word.

1- Who talks to us?

The Doctor? The wounded Lamb on the Cross, the Christ of the Heavenly Bread. He is meek and humble: we need to reach the level of His humility in order to be able listen to Him.

2- Crossing

If the "begging" requires determination, perseverance, and a movement of coming out of ourselves (senses, feelings, thoughts), receiving the Humble Medicine, the Meek Word of God requires humility and gentleness, coming out of ourselves, to be in a place where we can freely meet the Lord who is coming gently to meet us and talk to us.

The direct and personal action of the Holy Spirit does not occur in a powerful noise or earthquake, it comes as a gentle breeze. See Elijah's text to understand true contemplation and the action of the Holy Spirit:

"The Lord said, "Go out and stand on the mountain in the presence of the Lord, for the Lord is about to pass by."
Then a great and powerful wind tore the mountains apart and shattered the rocks before the Lord, but the Lord was not in the wind.
After the wind there was an earthquake, but the Lord was not in the earthquake.
After the earthquake came a fire, but the Lord was not in the fire.

And after the fire came a gentle whisper. When Elijah heard it, he pulled his cloak over his face and went out and stood at the mouth of the cave." "(1 Kings 19:11-13)

We expect God's daily Word to us to be like a powerful wind that will move us, or an earthquake that will shake us, or a fire that will burn us. In fact, God's Word and God's ways are more gentle, like a gentle whisper... not forcing us, suggesting, offering, inviting. God's meekness and gentleness is manifest in the way He communicates with us and in the contents itself of his Word and indication.

We expect power and we find gentleness, and as a consequence we might have a doubt: can it be God? Can this whisper be coming from God?

When God deals with us He does not force us, He does not exercise any violence on us. On the contrary, we need to be seduced, convinced from within, with the gentle breeze of his Word.

So, from the "violence" described previously (see above, on the act of humility) a violence that we exert upon ourselves, we do expect gentleness. From the power we use to humble ourselves, we reach the area in us where we can hear God's Whisper in his Word.

Therefore we Need to Understand

We need to come out of what attracts our senses, what captivates our emotions and what occupies our thoughts, all elements that can become tools of an attitude where we are the centre of everything. By contrast in order to listen to Jesus, we need to come out of ourselves, gaze at Him, focus on his face and wait for His Mouth which is ready to speak.

This movement of coming out of a something we can sense, feel or see in our mind or imagination, can cost us some serious effort - choosing Him, and repeating the act, can be our daily challenge... In this way we conquer the necessary freedom to be face to face with Jesus, free to listen to Him: this could be the meekness that is needed to meet Jesus!

This could be seen as a paradox, having this fine tuning between on the one hand effort, tension, strong determination, and on the other hand humility, gentleness, whisper, receptivity, true freedom.

IV- St James Explains *Lectio Divina*

In his beautiful letter, St. James explains *Lectio Divina* and its conditions to us. "Know this, my beloved brethren. Let every man be quick to hear, slow to speak, slow to anger, for the anger of man does not work the righteousness of God. Therefore put away all filthiness and rank growth of wickedness and receive with meekness the implanted word, which is able to save your souls. But be doers of the word, and not hearers only, deceiving yourselves. For if any one is a hearer of the word and not a doer, he is like a man who observes his natural face in a mirror; for he observes himself and goes away and at once forgets what he was like. But he who looks into the perfect law, the law of liberty, and perseveres, being no hearer that forgets but a doer that acts, he shall be blessed in his doing. If any one thinks he is religious, and does not bridle his tongue but deceives his heart, this man's religion is vain. Religion that is pure and undefiled before God and the Father is this: to visit orphans and widows in their affliction, and to keep oneself unstained from the world." (James 1:19-27)

Let us see how this presentation of *Lectio Divina* goes and let us discover a deeper understanding of this outstanding analysis of *Lectio Divina*.

Lectio Divina is about listening to Jesus' Word for us every day. Can we really listen to him? Should we prepare our heart in order to become able to listen?

Original Deafness

First and foremost it is important to remember that with the Fall (the Original Sin) we lose the capacity to listen and speak directly to God.

Moses is one of the first human beings to speak directly to God, face to face. People were scared of God.

Sin separates us from God, and radical grave sin, stops us from hearing, and hardens our heart. We need a deep operation that will transform our heart of stone into the heart of flesh.

This is why Jesus will perform a very important act on the Cross: He will open our "hearing" and our "speech" (capacity to talk), so that we will become, for the first time capable of directly hearing the Word of God and of talking to God directly and personally.

Even if this event occurs during Jesus' ministry, it occurs centrally on the Cross where Jesus accomplishes our Redemption, this is why Jesus has this deep sigh:

*"31 Then he returned from the region of Tyre, and went through Sidon to the Sea of Galilee, through the region of the Decapolis. 32 And they brought to him a man who was deaf and had an impediment in his speech; and they besought him to lay his hand upon him. 33 And taking him aside from the multitude privately, he put his fingers into his ears, and he spat and touched his tongue; 34 and looking up to heaven, he **sighed**, and said to him, "Ephphatha," that is, "Be opened." 35 And his ears were opened, his tongue was released, and he spoke plainly. 36 And he charged them to tell no one; but the more he charged them, the more zealously they proclaimed it. 37 And they were astonished beyond measure, saying, "He has done all things well; he even makes the deaf hear and the dumb speak.""* (Mark 7:31-37)

On the Cross Jesus brings us back from our darkness, our deafness, to the fluency of communication with God (listening-speaking). It is on the Cross that Jesus opens us up to God, changes us, gives us a new heart, a heart of flesh (Ezekiel 36:26), (like Mary's heart), capable of listening. *"Give thy servant therefore a heart that listens"* (1 Kings 3:9).

The Old Man in us, by definition is incapable of listening. This is why among many other rites, during Baptism, the Minister performs that same act that Jesus did and touches the ears of the person who is being baptised and his or her mouth, saying after Jesus: "Ephphatha" that is: "be opened".

Thus, when we sit down, in order to listen to Jesus, we need to remember that listening to Him is a Grace, not something obvious and automatic. This is why Jesus gives us a very special Grace of the Holy Spirit, in order for us to listen to Him, hear his voice, see Him in the Scriptures: He *"opened their minds to understand the Scriptures"* (Luke 24:45). Without this supernatural intervention of Jesus in our mind/heart, we cannot really hear Him, see Him, be touched by his words deeply, be moved by them.

To reiterate, it is important to acknowledge that we cannot take *Lectio Divina* (listening to Jesus) for granted, and that it is a huge Grace that we need to ask for humbly and insistently.

Note: For these reasons Mary is considered by Luke to be the only one who was capable of Listening to the Word of God, of obeying it, and of putting it into practice. This is why we need her, the New Eve, our Mother, to generate our new heart in the image of her heart, capable of listening and putting into practice Jesus' Words.

Impurity Makes us Deaf

St. James will explain some of the dispositions needed in order to become capable of listening to Jesus-God:

"Know this, my beloved brethren. Let every man be quick to hear, slow to speak, slow to anger, 20 for the anger of man does not work the righteousness of God." (James 1:19)

The goal is to become "quick to hear". In order to do so, there are many other workings of our soul (mind and will) that should cease: speaking and being angry to begin with. "Chatter" or gossip, for example, could be an expression of anger. Surely we cannot at the same time hate somebody and want to listen to Jesus? The reason can be seen when we realise that "hating" is an act of inner silent speech, where with our thoughts we direct the arrows of our anger against a particular person. The word of Jesus thereby, fails to have space in us.

It is illogical to expect two things that are opposite to dwell in us: anger and God's action in us. "Anger", too, can take many forms in us. Frustration for instance can makes us angry.

The Word of God needs and awaits a clean heart. There is a cleanness that we only can perform, which is our personal responsibility, that is, to refuse to surrender to anger and to ask God to give us a new heart, a heart of flesh, a heart "quick to hear".

"21 Therefore put away all filthiness and rank growth of wickedness and receive with meekness the implanted Word, which is able to save your souls."

As the above words indicate, St. James clarifies his thought by explaining for us that "anger" is for him any *"filthiness and rank growth of wickedness"*. If we want to receive the "implanted Word" of Jesus, we need to put away all what goes against it. Remember the thorns in the third soil in the Parable of the Sower? It has thorns that suffocate the Word of Jesus implanted in us. These thorns are all that is against the Word of God, all the desires that are not "the desire of God" (richness, worries,…).

God wants to save us. He has two means for doing so: His Word (his preaching), and His Body and Blood (the Cross). Jesus' word is capable of Saving our soul, changing it, purifying it, helping it to walk the path from the land of darkness to God who is Light and Love. God's Word is powerful, and we need it every day so that we can be saved: each day carries its effort with it, and each day has its own Bread, for man does not live on Bread alone but on the Real Bread: Jesus' Words.

"A heart quick to hear give me O Lord! A meek heart."

Putting into Practice

One of the characteristics of the heart that can receive the word of God is the heart that from the beginning is ready to put it into practice - unconditionally ready for this. We know that God can fulfil any Word He says to us. So why are we doubting God? We need to trust Him, trust that He knows what is best for us today, trust that we are his children, his dearest children, and that He wants to "save our souls" with his Word.

Do we really believe that we need to be saved, that is, changed by Him, by his words? Do we really entrust our being into the Hands of Jesus who then will give us each day a Word of Salvation, of change, of transformation, purification? Do we really see Jesus as our doctor, healer? Do we acknowledge the existence of this Grace every day? Are we following Jesus every day?

So, from start, the process of "listening" bears in it the deep determination to put into practice what we will hear from Jesus, we must be totally open to Him: "be doers of the word, and not hearers only, deceiving yourselves."

Being in front of Jesus is being in front of THE Truth, the truth about us. We expose ourselves to His Light. Wanting to listen to Jesus means that we want to see ourselves in Him: He sheds a light per day on us, reflects it to us, shows it to us. "For if anyone is a hearer of the word and not a doer, he is like a man who observes his natural face in a mirror" (James 1:23).

Jesus is our Divine Mirror

Therefore, it must be stressed that it is imperative that we to finish the entire process of listening, that is, listening and putting into practice.

Otherwise: *"he observes himself and goes away and at once forgets what he was like"* (James 1:24)

Really we need to be those who listen and put into practice the daily word of Jesus. This is what characterises us. We believe in the Incarnation, and part of the Incarnation is the incarnation of Jesus' words in us. This incarnation really changes our life, modifies it radically. This is a fundamental criterion of discernment. One can claim that he or she has a life of prayer, but it can be profoundly false. We cannot deceive God by just praying and doing various sacred acts of worship. If the Word of Jesus does not become incarnate in us, our worship is superficial, not made "in Spirit and in Truth", and we are just worshipping Jesus with our words, and body, but our heart does not listen to Him, is not guided by Him and is not transformed by His Word. *"This people honours me with their lips, but their heart is far from me; in vain do they worship me, teaching as doctrines the precepts of men"* (Matthew 15:8-9)

Jesus is our living Law, Jesus is our living example and guide. He is our Way. Jesus came to free us from the darkness, bringing us to the Light and transforming our inner being into His Light.

"But he who looks into the perfect Law, the law of liberty, and perseveres, being no hearer that forgets but a doer that acts, he shall be blessed in his doing." (James 1:25)

Perseverance is of the essence: otherwise our worship becomes false, superficial, pharisaic. How can we continue to have a heart that fails to listen to Jesus, and is not moved by his words if from our heart come all sorts of unworthy thoughts and silent acts?

"If any one thinks he is religious, and does not bridle his tongue but deceives his heart, this man's religion is vain." (James 1:26)

One can say: but what will Jesus ask me to do? Love Jesus' Body:

"He who says he is in the light and hates his brother is in the darkness still. 10 He who loves his brother abides in the light, and in it there is no cause for stumbling. 11 But he who hates his brother is in the darkness and walks in the darkness, and does not know where he is going, because the darkness has blinded his eyes." (1 John 2:9-11) *"he who does not love his brother whom he has seen, cannot love God whom he has not seen"* (1 John 4:20)

Who are the most vulnerable people on earth according to biblical tradition? Those who have nobody on earth to take care of them? The orphans and the widows? These are the most "poor" persons. Before reaching them, however, we need to open ourselves up to the people closest to us, followed afterwards by our going deeper and deeper into Jesus' Body until we reach the poorest of the poor: *"Religion that is pure and undefiled before God and the Father is this: to visit orphans and widows in their affliction, and to keep oneself unstained from the world."* (James 1:27) "Religion" is worship, is to love God, is all the acts of worship. It is giving what we have, who we are, letting the love of God flow from Him, through our heart to the poor, Jesus' Body, is really one of the deepest and most powerful ways of "putting into practice" Jesus' Word: *Lectio Divina.*

Conclusion

Expressed simply it means we really need to meditate upon these few verses of St James' letter, in order to deepen our understanding of *Lectio Divina.*

St. James Explains *Lectio Divina* 2

In the second chapter of his letter (James 2:14-26), St. James continues to explain to us what *Lectio Divina* is.

The Act of Faith is to Receive a Word

What is faith then? Our understanding today of "faith" might not be the one meant in various passages in the Bible. Plus, each author in the Bible, makes some aspect of "faith" shine out. So we might feel that we have different versions of the same topic, but in fact these are only different angles that allow us to better grasp that spiritual reality of faith and its act.

For many authors of the Bible, faith is an act that allows us to receive a Word from God, and to put it into practice. By this act, we open ourselves to God's word/message, and we offer a space for it in ourselves (in our existence, in our body, our soul,..), so that that word can "become flesh" in us.

The best example that illustrates the act of faith is Mary in the Annunciation. Here the Angel of God is transmitting to Mary a Word from God, a Message from God. Mary does not immediately say "yes", bypassing her mind. On the contrary she makes the effort, with her mind, to understand what that Message clearly means, discovering by doing so, the exact part she is about to play in allowing the word of God to become flesh in her heart and in her flesh. Only then does she say: yes, here I am, with all my being, offered to God, and to this word that He has uttered to me.

For this reason, Mary is praised, and Zechariah, who also received a celestial message, by contrast is blamed. The exact reason, therefore, why Mary is called "blessed" is because she believed that if God utters a word (a message) He can fulfil his Word : "blessed is she who believed that there would be a fulfilment of what was spoken to her from the Lord." (Luke 1:45) The Angel Gabriel explains to her the exact point of Faith: "no word [uttered by God] is impossible, to [be realised by] God". (Luke 1:37). The majority of the translations say: "for nothing is impossible to God", which is not what the text says and is not Luke's purpose: in fact he wants to explain the mechanism of Faith.

How Faith is Transmitted to Us

By Jesus' Redemption on the Cross, we receive the Grace of Faith i.e. the capacity to open up to the Word of God. By Jesus' Redemption, Mary was able to say "yes" to the Angel (see the Mystery of the Immaculate Conception). By Jesus' Redemption, and through his Plan, He wanted Mary to be at one and the same time our Role model (Archetype of the perfect Disciple of Jesus) and our Mother (the one that generates us into God's Life). Jesus made Mary and Mary's "yes" (the "Yes" of her entire being) capable of holding our "yes". By the "Yes" of Mary, we receive the Grace, in our turn, to hear a Word coming from God, understand our part in its incarnation, and say "yes" to it, like Mary, and in Mary. This is the full extent of the Act of Faith. This is why Mary is praised this way: "Blessed are you among women" (Luke 1:42) (we are all, through her, capable of conceiving God's will, a word from Him each day). What do we conceive? "blessed is the fruit of your womb": Jesus! This is why "all generations will call [her] blessed" (Luke 1:48). Because all generations will go to her (as our mother) to draw from her the capacity to receive the word of God (to believe, to have faith).

St. James Explains the Act of Faith

God's word for us is to love God and to love our neighbour. So Faith will entail putting that word into practice. With this understanding of faith, let us read St. James' passage:

81

"What does it profit, my brethren, if a man says he has faith but has not works/acts? Can his faith save him? If a brother or sister is ill-clad and in lack of daily food, and one of you says to them, "Go in peace, be warmed and filled," without giving them the things needed for the body, what does it profit? So faith by itself, if it has no works, is dead." (James 2:14-17)

Having faith itself, that is having the capacity to say "yes" to a word sent by God to us, is a grace. But exercising faith, is something that is essential. Faith is not passive. It is a grace, a Talent to be implemented, activated, invested in. Imagine Mary not saying "yes" to God, and not receiving Him in her! The fact that she is the "Immaculate Conception" gives her Faith the capacity to say "yes", the capacity to "conceive the word" in her heart and in her womb. But if she fails to say yes, if she fails to use that faith, then nothing will happen. There will be no fruitfulness.

If we do not say "yes" to the word of God, if we do not receive into our life, in our flesh that "word", if we do not give it a space within us, what is then "faith"? Have we allowed the grace of faith to be enacted in us?

St. James continues: "But some one will say, "You have faith and I have works/acts." Show me your faith apart from your works/acts, and I by my works/acts will show you my faith." (James 2:18)

The Act of Faith is the capacity to receive a word from God and to give it our flesh.

"You believe that God is one; you do well. Even the demons believe — and shudder. Do you want to be shown, you shallow man, that faith apart from works/acts is barren? Was not Abraham our father justified by works, when he offered his son Isaac upon the altar? You see that faith was active along with his works/acts, and faith was completed by works/acts, and the scripture was fulfilled which says, "Abraham believed God, and it was reckoned to him as righteousness"; and he was called the friend of God. You see that a man is justified by works/acts and not by faith alone. And in the same way was not also Rahab the harlot justified by works/acts when she received the messengers and sent them out another way? For as the body apart from the spirit is dead, so faith apart from works is dead." (James 2:19-26)

Faith as a grace is one thing, and the act of faith is something different: it is to receive a word from God and "incarnate" it. "blessed is she who believed that there would be a fulfilment of the word that was spoken to her from the Lord." (Luke 1:45)

The Total Gift of Ourselves to God

It is true as well, that one has to offer oneself totally to God when he makes his act of Faith. Let us contemplate Mary: she does not say an intellectual abstract "yes" to God. She commits totally to Him, she puts all her life into God's hands, and commits to his Word. This is the condition that will allow the Word of God to come into her heart and into her womb.

In order to see God we need to give ourselves totally to God, and this is purity, a purity that we can enact (with the Grace of God).

If we "lose our life" by giving it to God, we get everything: God, and all the rest. Seek the kingdom of God first, and all the rest will be given to you for free.

Purity is the condition of success in *Lectio Divina*: offering ourselves to God, completely, unconditionally,… this is the only way to receive God. If we give everything to Him, we get everything (Him).

Conclusion

Lectio Divina is a real act of Living Faith where we listen to a word coming from God to us, where we offer ourselves to God totally and where God incarnates his word in us. Very much like in the Annunciation.

St. James Explains *Lectio Divina* 3

Not Committing Mistakes in What we Say

"if any one makes no mistakes in what he says he is a perfect man, able to bridle the whole body also" (James 3:2). What is the perfect man? The man who has synergy occurring perfectly, synergy between God's action in him and his action. This means that he has been purified and transformed in Jesus, so he becomes docile to the Holy Spirit: Jesus lives in him, so all what comes from his thoughts, and out of his mouth, is coming from this harmonious collaboration between Jesus and him.

This means that *Lectio Divina* transforms him, word by word, brick by brick, until Jesus becomes alive in Him and starts to move him with his Spirit.

Lectio Divina is meant to change the soul, act by act, part by part, step by step. One word after the other from Jesus transforms our being in Him so that He becomes alive in us. In fact each word received burns, transforms that part of the soul that produces that act into a 'portion' of Jesus himself.

"Perfection" is obviously expressed in all sorts of different ways, but the easiest and most palpable way to notice it is in speech. What comes out of the mouth, comes from the abundance of what is in the heart says Jesus (see Matthew 12:34). Speech reveals what is at the root of the human being, his heart. The quality of the speech (and first thoughts) reveals the perfection of the person.

In his third piece of advice to a religious "against the world" (the world with its thoughts and behaviour is considered one of the enemies of the soul), St. John of the Cross quotes St. James: *"If any one thinks he is religious, and does not bridle his tongue but deceives his heart, this man's religion is vain"* (James 1:26) which is close to the initial quote:

"if any one makes no mistakes in what he says he is a perfect man, able to bridle the whole body also" (James 3:2), but he explains it saying: *"This is applicable to the interior, quite as much as to the exterior tongue – to thoughts as well as words."*

From Three Tents to One Tent

The Mystery of the Transfiguration reveals much about *Lectio Divina*.

Let us remember that the early Christian liturgy took the Liturgy of the Word from the Synagogue (from the Sabbath) then added to it the Gospel and a letter from the New Testament. We have a trace of this structure in the actual Syriac Orthodox Church Liturgy. So this means, we have: one reading from the Torah (Moses) and one reading from the Prophets (Elijah) together with readings about Jesus (Gospel and a letter from the New Testament).

When we listen to this liturgy, we have the impression that the three or more readings are three distinct texts, bearing three different messages. We tend to say with Peter: "Master, it is well that we are here; let us make three tents, one for you and one for Moses and one for Elijah." (Mark 9:5) In fact, this is a clear indication of the sacramental challenge of the Liturgy of the Word. We need to ask ourselves: To whom are we listening? Why do we still have a reading from Moses and another from the Prophets (Elijah)? Do we have three texts, therefore three messages?

In fact the supernatural action of God during the Liturgy of the Word is essentially led by Jesus himself.

Peter sees division, and offers to build three tents, according to his initial perception.

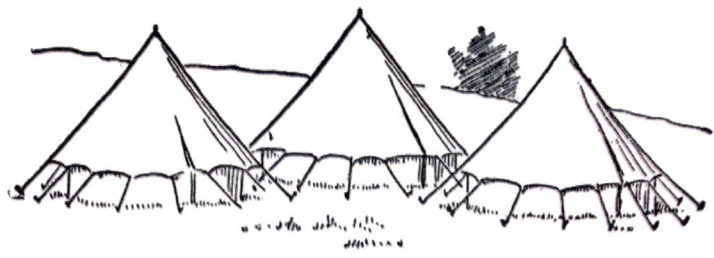

But then, the supernatural action of the Father is innitiated: a Cloud will overshadow them, and the one and only voice of the one and only God the Father will be heard, and it will draw attention to Jesus only. "And a cloud overshadowed them, and a voice came out of the cloud, "This is my beloved Son; listen to him." Would this exclude Moses and Elijah? On the contrary, it will unify everything under one, and only one Tent: Jesus himself: "And suddenly looking around they no longer saw any one with them but Jesus only".

Here is how John will tell us about the Transfiguration: "And the Word became flesh and pitched his Tent among us, full of grace and truth; we saw his glory, glory as of the only Son from the Father"(John 1:14).

So, the action of the Father is to 'speak' his Son to us and in us, to utter his Word (the Son) to us, asking us to listen essentially only to Him. The overshadowing of the Divine Luminous Cloud has this effect, to put us all under the only Tent of the Son. So, in the end, instead of seeing Moses and Elijah with Him, we see only Him.

Even if we have two or three texts in *Lectio Divina*, in fact, it is one Light that we receive, one message, for it is Jesus alone who is speaking to us.

We have the same experience every day that Peter had: initially seeing two or three texts, and finally, with the Power of the Holy Spirit (the Divine Cloud), seeing only Jesus, the one and only Divine Tent.

In sum, the initial questions we asked ourselves have the following answers:

– To whom are we listening during the Liturgy of the Word, when we read the Torah (Pentateuch) and the Prophets? – We are listening to Jesus. Because the Liturgy of the Word is about Him wanting to speak to us.

86

– Why do we still have a Reading from Moses and another from the Prophets (Elijah)? – We have them because the Old Testament is the Word of God, and as we see in Luke 24, there is a very important experience we need to undergo, by the Power of the Holy Spirit: Jesus needs to open our mind, and therefore we are enabled to see Him in the Old Testament: a Transfiguration of the Text of the Old Testament happens, and its letter (like Jesus clothes) is transfigured, and we start to see his Face in the text of the Old Testament.

– Do we have three texts, therefore three messages? – We have three texts, but only one message given by Jesus to us, one Tent remains: Jesus' Tent, because He is the only begotten Son of the Father and He came to talk to us and give us his words that are Spirit and Life, Holy Spirit and Divine Life.

Become a "Doctor"

St. James has this piece of advice for us: *"Only a few of you, my brothers, should be **teachers/doctors**, bearing in mind that we shall receive a stricter judgement."* (James 3:1) How does this apply to *Lectio Divina*?

Lectio Divina is not about accumulating knowledge on the Bible. It is not about knowing or studying the Bible. It is about listening to Jesus, through the Bible. The difference is huge. In extreme cases, one can have a PhD in Bible (Exegesis) and not be doing one single *Lectio Divina*.

The one speaks to the mind only, leaves it to itself. The other speaks to the will (the whole person), through the mind. Of course it is better to have both, since it helps. But if the amount of knowledge exceeds the amount of "digested" light, it damages more than it helps.

The digested light is the light that we receive in *Lectio,* and which becomes flesh in us. This is the listening process made complete (listening and putting into practice). The "non digested light" is the one we contemplate like in a mirror, and then leave it and forget: *"Anyone who listens to the Word and takes no action is like someone who looks at his own features in a mirror and, once he has seen what he looks like, goes off and immediately forgets it."* (James 1:23-24)

Accumulating knowledge without digesting it, with only knowledge and no practical experience is "becoming a doctor/teacher" the wrong way. It is like greed. One listens but no action is taken.

Lectio Divina reminds us of the correct use of the mind. It is not against learning, studying, but it just warns us, like St. James, that the more we accumulate (like in greed) the more we have to give account. That word that we accumulate without putting into practice is already judging us.

Lectio Divina brings wisdom to a frenetic mind. The majority of us have a frenetic mind, wanting to know, but not applying what we learn. The Word of God, source of knowledge on God, on us, is not always used for that purpose: improving ourselves.

"The same tongue"

St. James says: *"the blessing and curse come out of the same mouth/tongue"* (James 3:10). How does this affect our understanding and our practice of *Lectio Divina*? As we have seen above, there is an "inner tongue", that is, our mind produces thoughts. The mind (encouraged by the will) is the main faculty that deals with the *Lectio*, in the sense that we need to have a clear understanding of Jesus' will. The mind is sacred and should serve the lord…

What the mind and will produce (the inner tongue) require great attention from us and vigilance.

Our inner speech, our inner acts (acts of the mind and will) are very important. St. James is inviting us to watch our acts, the roots of our acts. Only God sees our inner "tongue"... but our inner "tongue" is our judge: watch carefully how you judge things: if you have mercy, mercy will be done to you. The same way you judge people and things will be applied to you.

Great vigilance should be applied to the thoughts and inner acts that we produce, and they should be full of God's Grace: Mercy, Compassion, practising Spiritual Hospitality (receiving everybody, unconditionally, in our heart).

Printed in Great Britain
by Amazon

47892172R00050